FOUL DEEDS AND SUSPICIOUS DEATHS IN YORK

Foul Deeds and Suspicious Deaths In
YORK

KEITH HENSON

Series Editor
Brian Elliott

Wharncliffe Books

For CJ, Paige and Willa
Thanks for the patience.

All the wickedness of the world is print to him.
Mrs Gamp in The Life and Adventures of Martin Chuzzelwit
(Charles Dickens)

First Published in 2003 by
Wharncliffe Books
an imprint of
Pen and Sword Books Limited,
47 Church Street, Barnsley,
South Yorkshire. S70 2AS

Copyright © Keith Henson 2003

For up-to-date information on other titles produced under the
Wharncliffe imprint, please telephone or write to:

> **Wharncliffe Books**
> **FREEPOST**
> **47 Church Street**
> **Barnsley**
> **South Yorkshire S70 2BR**
> **Telephone (24 hours): 01226 734555**

ISBN: 1-903425-33-6

A CIP catalogue record of this book is available from the
British Library

Cover illustration: *Front – The Author in York.* Paige and Willa Henson
Back – The Shambles, c.1900. Author's collection

Printed in the United Kingdom by
CPI UK

Contents

Chapter 1   The Where and The How 7

Chapter 2   Money and Rope 17

Chapter 3   Jonathon Martin and the Art of Insane Arson 29

Chapter 4   The Asylum 39

Chapter 5   A Child Called Hannah 49

Chapter 6   The Horsefair Murder 57

Chapter 7   Unhappy Families 63

Chapter 8   A Policeman's Lot 71

Chapter 9   Poor Horatio 83

Chapter 10 Murder on Hope Street 93

Chapter 11 The Killing of John Dalby 101

Chapter 12 The Mystery at $5^{1}/_{2}$ 109

Chapter 13 A Village Tragedy 121

Chapter 14 The Prevention of Cruelty 135

Chapter 15 Almost Death by Chocolate 155

Chapter 16 Who Killed Norma Dale? 167

Sources, Bibliography and Acknowledgements 174

Index 175

York's Guildhall, for centuries the centre of local government and justice. The Author

Chapter 1

The Where and The How

A Brief Look at Capital Punishment

There is a story that tells of a shipwrecked mariner, who, having been washed ashore, scrambles up a cliff in search of help. The first sight that greets him is the stark silhouette of a gallows scaffold and the mariner falls to his knees and thanks God that he finds himself in a Christian country. In England, he would not have had far to travel to find more of these Christian symbols. The country had embraced Saxon King Athelstan's decree that said – 'Let him be smitten so that his neck breaks', and in those early days the punishment was as likely to be carried out by men of the cloth as any government.

Among the franchises granted to the monasteries in the thirteenth and fourteenth centuries is one that reads *Furca et Fossa,* in other words 'Gallows and Pit.' The rope for a man; the pit of water for drowning a woman. The Abbots gave with one hand and took with the other. Bound by church law to offer refuge for nine days to thieves, they were most likely to be the ones to hang them also. The privilege of *infanthief,* that is to punish those found guilty of stealing, nearly always resulted in hanging, regardless of the value of the stolen item.

The church court at York dealt with the most serious of cases and the Archbishop had a gallows erected on the Foss Bridge in the thirteenth century, while the Dean and Chapter operated a structure at the junction of the Wiggington and Haxby roads, where Clarence Gardens stand today. The Abbott of St Mary's handed out punishment from a scaffold on the road known today as Burton Stone Lane and it was his inefficient operation that prompted the bailiffs of York to construct a scaffold of their own, to the south of the city on a stretch of common land called the Knavesmire. It was completed on 7 March 1379 and they gave it a name synonymous with executions in London since the thirteenth century – Tyburn.

It became a name to be feared, both in the north and the

The ruins of St Mary's Abbey. The Author

This plain stone marks the site of the Tyburn gallows. The Author

south and many a thief and murderer ended his days swinging from a rope on the Knavesmire. Some of York's most enduring images arose from that place. Such as John Nevison, the 'Gentleman Highwayman', bound in chains, claiming the King's pardon in vain and Dick Turpin offering an ivory whistle to his executioner before leaping from the cart to his death. One who inspired both poets and novelists was Eugene Aram, the famous murderer of Knaresborough, who was taken half dead to swing from the Three-legged Mare, as the tri-cornered scaffold became known.

Public hangings were good excuses for an unofficial public holiday and men such as Aram, who went in taciturn acceptance were seen as poor sports. Having followed the procession of the condemned prisoner from the castle and having seen their souls strengthened and tongues loosened by landlords along the way, what they expected was some participation. Confession was

The grave stone of Dick Turpin, Tyburn's most famous customer. The Author

always popular, both with the authorities and the public. For those who had sent the man to his death it was vindication of their decision and for the public a salacious confession was considered fine entertainment. Playful banter, cursing, weeping, it was a performance that was needed and some would regale their audience with rousing speeches of farewell.

Spectators able to read could purchase one of the chapbooks sold by the many hawkers who frequented the event in company with the ballad sellers. Cheaper than newspapers, at a penny a time, they told the felon's tale in a manner sure to enthral, with little regard to the facts of the case. Later, the day's events would be re-enacted for money in the alehouse yards by groups of actors, with the most popular of these being the one attended by the hangman and his associates.

When horse racing came to the Knavesmire in 1731, executions would coincide with race days, creating festivals of sport and death. The city's bawdy, brawling society could fill their day with both, and from John Carr's grandstand, built in 1754, ten thousand of them were guaranteed a good view.

In 1801 it was those very people, the racegoers and coach travellers, who finally brought about Tyburn's demise. These new, seemingly compassionate and religious members of grand society objected to having the grisly sight forced upon them. The last hanging at Tyburn was, like its first, a soldier found guilty of rape. Edward Hughes, who served with the 18th Light Dragoons, had his date with the rope on 29 August 1801. In the April of that year the *York Herald* ran this report:

> *The plan some time ago recommended by Major Topham for altering the place of execution at this city, is, we understand, now likely to be adopted... it cannot be otherwise than desirable that the public business of the city, the feeling of the humane, and the*

The view across the Knavesmire from Tyburn. The Author

entrance of the town should no longer be annoyed by dragging criminals through the streets.

A new scaffold was built at the rear of the gaol and with fervent imagination they called it, The New Drop. Prisoners could now walk straight from the condemned cell to the scaffold:

Thus will be removed from one of the principle roads leading to the city that disagreeable nuisance, the gallows. York Herald

It was still open to the public, only now the delicate eyes of York's elegant gents and ladies would not be forced to view its spectacle – unless, of course, they chose to. Many did, because it was necessary to widen Castlegate Postern to a width of eight metres to allow for public viewing.

By the 1850s society began to turn against these public dispatches (even so, 9 August 1856 saw the biggest ever gathering for an execution at the New Drop when a crowd, in excess of 15,000, watched William Dove hang for the murder of his wife in Leeds). Charles Dickens, a regular visitor to York, wrote that 'public hanging was a wicked and fruitless act of vengeance.' Murderers fascinated him, but after seeing an execution outside Horsemonger prison in London he wrote to *The Times* and spoke of his disgust at the 'screeching and laughing' of the ghoulish crowd. He demanded that public executions should cease and take place behind prison walls. As he put it, they should be carried out in 'holes and corners.'

Another observer of the time, a barrister by the name of Charles Phillips, who served as a commissioner in the Court of Insolvent Debtors, wrote in 1856:

We hanged for anything – for a shilling – for five pounds – for cattle – for coining – for forgery, even witchcraft – for things that were and things that could not be.

And he was right. During the Tudor reign no more than fifty offences carried the death penalty, but by the 1820s there were more than two hundred. Following an act of Parliament in 1868 public executions at the New Drop came to an end with the hanging of Frederick Parker, who, having been released from Beverley prison, killed his companion, Daniel Driscol, with a hedge stake.

From that point on, the only visible sign to the people of the city would be a black flag hoisted above Clifford's Tower at the time of execution. Interest in such an uneventful exhibition waned and when Edward Wheatfill met with the hangman, William Marwood, in 1882, the *Yorkshire Gazette* reported that,

> *The execution attracted no public interest whatever. No persons congregated in groups outside the castle walls and the appearance of Tower Street was the same as usual. Never did a private execution pass off so quietly in York before.*

The York Assizes passed their final sentence of death in 1896.

Hanging, as a means of punishment, was by no means the only one handed down in York's history. The city's most beloved Saint, Margaret Clitherow, was forced to undergo the process known as *Piene forte et dure*. Reserved exclusively for those who refused to plead to the charges laid before them, it consisted of pegging the accused spread-eagled upon the floor with a sharp stone beneath their back. Then a board was placed on top of them and one by one heavy stones loaded on to it until, unable to bear the crushing weight, the poor soul finally answered the charge. It was not so much a form of punishment as one of torture and it nearly always resulted in death. In 1580, Margaret Clitherow, a butcher's wife from the Shambles, had been accused of harbouring Catholic priests and promoting the teaching of that faith; both against the laws of Elizabeth's Protestant England. She would not answer the charges put before her, because in her own mind she had no charges to

Clifford's Tower. The Author

The present day Shambles is a tourist heaven. Margaret Clitherow's house is on the left. The Author

respond to. After being deprived of food and allowed only 'puddle water' for her thirst, she was taken to the Toll Booth on the Ouse Bridge, where she was crushed beneath eight hundredweight of rock, causing her ribs to break through the skin. In her final words she called for the mercy of her Lord. The whole process took fifteen minutes.

Another to receive this penance was Walter Calverly of Calverly Hall, who in the spring of 1605, in a fit of jealousy and madness, killed two of his sons and attempted also to kill his wife and newborn baby. At his trial hearing in York he refused to answer to the charge of murder, or rather he was unable to understand what he had done. In an effort to make him plead, he was pressed to death on 5 August 1605.

The pit of water, mentioned earlier, was for the drowning of women, but in later years a woman might expect to be dragged to the sight of execution and burnt where she lay. In the eighteenth century, if she was found guilty of *Petit Treason*, that is, the murder of her husband, then she could be chained to a stake and burnt. If luck were with her, then a compassionate hangman might successfully strangle her by means of a looped rope before the flames touched the skin. More civilised citizens, such as those of York, might choose to first hang the woman on the gallows before burning. On 25 March 1605, Elizabeth Cook was first hung on the scaffold at St Leonards and then had her body burnt and, in 1649, three women suffered in the same way at Tyburn. One of the most infamous examples of this punishment had taken place the previous year, in 1648, with the case of Isabella Billington. Along with her husband, she was found guilty of crucifying her mother and sacrificing a calf and a chicken, all in the name of Satan. As late as 1776, Elizabeth Bordington was put to the rope for the poisoning of her husband and was then burnt at the side of the Tadcaster Road on the Knavesmire. The practice was finally halted in 1799.

For those found guilty of treason, the retribution could be that of being Hung, Drawn and Quartered, or more correctly, Drawn, Hung and Quartered, and many of the sixteenth century northern rebels ended their days in such a manner. A fourteenth century statute describes the process in detail and was used in this and similar form for centuries after:

1. *That the aforesaid ... be drawn to the gallows*
[That is, dragged behind a horse.]
2. *He is there to be hanged by the neck, and let down alive.*
3. *His bowels are to be taken out.*
4. *And if he be alive, to be burnt.*
[The sudden shock of seeing ones insides removed before your eyes often ended the punishment earlier than intended, and an unskilled executioner might not help either.]
5. *His head is to be cut off.*
6. *His body is to be divided into four parts.*
7. *And his head and quarters are to be placed where our king shall direct.*

In York that place was Micklegate Bar, while other Yorkshire towns would vie for the remaining quarters to mount on their own walls and towers.

Perhaps the most famous to have their head set upon a spike on Micklegate Bar was Richard, Duke of York, following the Battle of Wakefield in 1460. Shakespeare immortalised the scene in Henry VI when Queen Margaret exclaims,

Off with his head and set it on York gates
So York may overlook the town of York.

Catholic martyr, 'Blessed' Sir Thomas Percy, The Earl of Northumberland, lost his head to Micklegate in 1572 for his part in the Northern Rebellion of 1569, just like his fighting forebear the great Sir Henry (Hotspur) Percy in 1403. Thomas's father had also hung at London's Tyburn in 1537 for his part in the Pilgrimage of Grace. Not for nothing did Yorkshiremen claim that if you dug down six feet in the county you would find a Percy.

The authorities expected these gruesome warnings to stand for many years, and so, the heads were often parboiled to preserve them and seasoned with cumin seed to deter the birds from picking at the flesh.

The last heads to look down from Micklegate were those of William Conolly and James Mayne after the Battle of Culloden in 1746. Twenty-one of their Jacobite comrades were buried behind the castle wall, but Mayne and Conolly stared out from

Blossom Street. Micklegate Bar greeted all those travelling north. Author's collection

their lofty perch until they were secretly removed on a January night in 1754. The York Corporation offered a reward of £10 for the capture of the perpetrator and even the King demanded to know who was responsible for this 'wicked, traitorous and outrageous proceeding.' In July of the same year, William Arundel, a tailor, was convicted and sentenced to two years and, if he failed to find £200 surety as to his good behaviour, two years more. On reflection, Arundel was lucky that *his* head did not become Micklegate's last incumbent.

Micklegate Bar. The Author

Chapter 2

Money and Rope

Two Tyburn Tales: 1800

Daniel Defoe once said that the gaol at York Castle was the finest in Europe. If that was the case, then God help the rest. Even John Wesley, visiting two inmates in 1759, wrote that he found it 'the most commodious prison.' Large it may have been, but it was overcrowded and filthy. When we read that Defoe found the situation 'high, pleasant and airy,' it sounds more like a hotel than a gaol. The buildings that we see today on the 'Eye of Yorkshire' are the former Debtor's Gaol, the Women's Prison and the County Assize Courts. The prisons are occupied by the famous Castle Museum, while the Court House is still in use to this day. In what is now a car park, stood a further prison building; built in 1826 it was unused by 1929 and finally demolished in 1935. The high and imposing prison walls, built in 1822, were also demolished in the same year. The only visible sign of the castle is the scarred remains of the keep,

The County Court (right) built in 1777 and the Debtor's Prison (left) completed in 1705. The Author

known as Clifford's Tower, a place that throughout its history has been the scene of execution and slaughter.

When Elizabeth Fry, the great prison reformer, visited the prison in the spring of 1819, her cousin, Joseph Gurney recorded the scene:

> *The prisoners are allowed one pound and a half of wheaten bread daily, and one shilling per week.... . From the squalid appearance of some of them, it seemed to us questionable whether the allowance of food was sufficient to maintain them in health; the apothecary of the prison, whom we saw, expressed an opinion that it was not.... . Several of them were extremely ill clad; two men without shirts.*

She made a number of recommendations for improvement, including the stopping of public access to the felons (prisoners sold goods in the courtyard), the supply of sufficient food and clothing, the improvement of cleanliness and the provision of employment and education, by which, 'They would have no time to corrupt either another or the public.' On her return visit in September 1819, she found that little had changed.

Warders were unpaid, earning their wage by selling to the inmates what meagre extras they could afford and prisoner's clothing was taken away and pawned. Rooms were devoid of

This view of York taken at the turn of the nineteenth century shows the prison walls still in place (centre right). Author's collection

YORK.

sunlight and people slept two or more to an iron mesh bed in a cell no larger than two meters square, often remaining locked in for sixteen hours at a time. Those kept chained in irons would polish the metal with their raw skin. In the sixteenth century, Catholic recusants were even charged for the use of these irons – ten shillings for a Yeoman, twenty shillings for a Gentleman and forty shillings for an Esquire. The weight of the manacles could exceed thirteen kilo's. For those who found enough food to survive there was the dreaded 'Gaol Fever' (Typhus) that raged in the unsanitary conditions.

The problem of alleviating boredom for the prisoners was solved by Sir William Cubit, the Suffolk engineer, in 1817, with the invention of the Treadwheel, and York, ever keen that the best in Europe should keep up with the times, installed its own. It consisted of a giant wooden wheel, set with a series of steps, twenty centimetres apart and separated by partitions. The prisoners would walk the steps and turn the wheel. It had no purpose other than the action of turning, as it provided no power to any machine. The monotonous, draining exercise, coupled with the lack of nourishment, broke many a man's spirit. When the Chartist, Samuel Holberry arrived into the terrible conditions of York Castle Prison in 1840, having endured hours upon the wheel at Northallerton, he died and the movement had its martyr. York removed its treadwheel in 1833.

During August of 1800, the prison of York held two inmates of very different circumstances: Elizabeth Johnson and John Curry. For both, the sight of the rope was beckoning at Tyburn; but for one, it was the start of a notorious career.

The war with France was affecting trade, pushing up prices and newly established income taxes. Able-bodied men were being drawn into the army and navy; although it has to be said that Yorkshire and its principle city had not rushed to volunteer. Metal for coinage was in short supply and those found guilty of being even associated with forgery found no sympathy with the hard-pressed citizens.

Elizabeth Johnson had resided in the gaol since 8 June, when she had been committed on the oath of Charles Methley. He swore that she had passed to him in Pontefract on the 7th, a forged £1 note, purporting to be that of the Bank of England,

The former Women's prison, built in 1780 and designed by the prolific John Carr of York. The Author

and two counterfeit half guineas. On her person she carried other false coinage, including seven, one-shilling pieces.

She finally walked into court on 9 August to face Justices, Sir Alan Chambre and Sir Robert Graham. There can be no doubt that Elizabeth had not forged the money herself. More likely, is that some rogue had forced it upon her in the street and made it clear what would happen if she spoke his name. She could afford no legal counsel, spoke no words of defence and made no plea while the good and the great decided her fate. She knew little of them and they cared nothing for her. It was an impressive roll call - Justice Chambre, circuit judge of Abbot Hall near Kendal who was close to being called to London; Sir Robert D'Arcy Hildyard of Whinstead, the last Baronet of his manor on Holderness; the educated and highly cultured Sir Thomas Gascoigne of Parlington Hall, near Aberford and Sir William Milner of Nun Appleton Hall, near Selby, a house that would later inspire poets – why should any of these men care.

Twenty prisoners had stood in the dock before Elizabeth took her turn; she was little more than an anonymous distraction, tainted with prison filth. Not until sentencing was being carried out did she break her silence.

The *York Herald's* summing up of proceedings that day clearly shows how those in authority and influence viewed Elizabeth Johnson:

The behaviour of this unfortunate woman, while the Judge was passing sentence, was wretched and furious in the extreme; so much so, that though repeatedly requested by his Lordship to be silent, she would not and he was therefore obliged to break off in the midst of an impressive address to her, and proceed to passing the awful sentence of the law; when she was immediately ordered from the court.

God forbid that this unfortunate woman should cry out when she saw Sir Alan don his black cap. Of course, the newspapers were never intended for the Elizabeth Johnson's of this world. They were relatively expensive and what were the chances of her being able to read? They were written for the erudite and sophisticated Chambre's, Hildyard's and Gascoignes to read in fashionable coffee houses and discuss in the weighty atmosphere of the Assembly Rooms – and it showed.

August 16 was race day on the Knavesmire:

Much company and great sport is expected at our races... the ground is in good condition, by being wetted by the late rains.

...Reported the press.

The only hanging for the day, Elizabeth, would provide no sport. Barely able to stand, mute and broken, she travelled on

The Assembly Rooms, opened in 1732 and designed by Lord Burlington. The Author

the cart from castle to scaffold. There would be no confession, no poignant farewell and no angry exchange with the crowd. The cart would come to a halt beneath the rope, and after it was placed beneath her chin and gently tightened, it would be driven away, leaving Elizabeth to be strangled until she died.

Many of those in the courtroom when sentencing was passed would have been at the racecourse. It is doubtful whether Miss Johnson interrupted their enjoyment.

Our second jailbird arrived at the castle the day before Elizabeth left. John Curry of Thirsk had been arrested for the theft of five sheep at Heworth, just outside the city walls and he too had received the death sentence from Justice Chambre. Unlike Elizabeth, John's meeting with the rope would be quite different.

John Curry (*aka* William Wilkinson) was born around the year 1770 and was described as a labourer. He first came to the notice of the courts in 1793, when he appeared at the spring assizes charged with the capital crime of sheep stealing.

It was alleged, that on 17-18 November 1792 he had stolen

The Old Herdsmen's Cottage, at the edge of the Heworth Stray. The Author

'one ewe sheep of the price of six shillings and five hog sheep of the price of three pounds.' The charge was never answered because John had already pleaded guilty to the theft of three ewes from William Smith, a Northallerton innkeeper. There could only be one sentence – death. Yet, somehow, he escaped the ultimate punishment when his sentence was commuted to seven years transportation. With the American colonies no longer in use following the War of Independence, John would spend his seven years dredging the River Thames aboard a prison ship.

He was given his freedom on 18 March 1800 and having survived such a tortuous time, might have been expected to settle to a crime-free life; but not for nothing was John's nickname 'Mutton Curry.' On 31 July he stole those five sheep from Thomas Severs of Heworth and found himself languishing in the gaol, having been escorted back from Lincolnshire.

At the spring assizes he admitted his guilt and again a death sentence was passed – and yet again commuted, on this occasion to fourteen years transportation. This time, however, there was to be a further twist when, with no given reason, the sentence was changed to one of fourteen years imprisonment in the castle prison.

While the rest of the country had handed the job of hanging the condemned to the Newgate executioner, York and Lancaster stood alone in enlisting the services of their own hangman. They had enough 'Gallow-Birds' from which to choose and this was exactly how the position was filled. Blackbourne, the man who hanged Turpin, had been due to hang for his own crimes, and likewise John Curry was coerced by the gaoler at the castle to take the job at the New Drop in 1802. His first employ was on 28 August with the hanging of William Barker, for the theft of a horse, William Jackson for burglary, and Thomas Roberts, ironically, for stealing sheep.

Why John took the position is unclear. According to sources at the time, he was 'under considerable obligations to the Gaoler,' but reports that his sentence was cut short are false, because, although now employed by the city, he stayed a prisoner until 1814.

His first job of note came with the dispatching of fourteen Luddite rioters on 16 January 1813, the largest number of hangings in a single day at the castle. Five of the men had taken

The gallows of the New Drop have been demolished, but the doors through which the condemned took their final steps remain in place. The Author

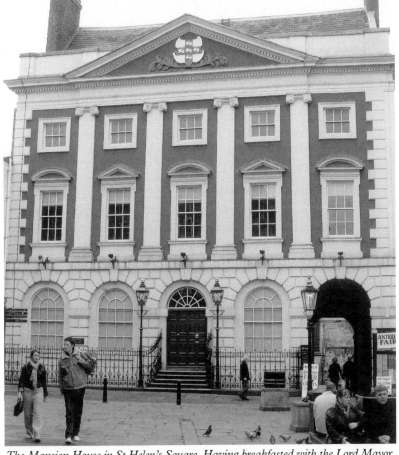

The Mansion House in St Helen's Square. Having breakfasted with the Lord Mayor, the Assize judges would be led in splendid procession to the courthouse.. The Author

part in the infamous attack on Cartwright's mill at Rawfolds (an incident related in Charlotte Bronte's, *Shirley*), three had been found guilty of murder and nine of theft, all on the word of spies and turncoats.

On the old three-beamed scaffold at Tyburn, hanging fourteen would have proved an easy task, but at the New Drop it required two sessions. Just before 11 am, seven of the condemned rioters were led out to the gallows. A huge crowd, held at bay by a line of soldiers, jostled for a view of these so-called Luddites. York's population had been swelled by cartloads of working class followers, in from the West Riding and Lancashire. Joseph Crowther, the rope at his neck, turned to them and shouted, 'Farewell, lads,' whereas John Hill called for his friends to 'Take warning by my fate,' much to the delight of all mill owners. At 1.30 pm another seven were dropped through the floor and Colonel Norton remarked that they did so 'praying most loudly.' Those, whose bodies were claimed by their families, were escorted by a host of sympathisers out of the city.

It can be no surprise that John Curry took to drinking. There is nothing to suggest that he enjoyed his work and as the *Yorkshire Gazette* pointed out...

> ...*it is to be much regretted that, whilst preparing the final noose for his unfortunate victims, Gin was apt to prove a snare to him, and that he could never be induced to adjust a Hempen Cord without an undue allowance of Blue Thread.*

And it was the 'Blue Thread' that brought about John's more colourful episodes.

On 14 April 1821, he had two executions to perform, one at the castle and the other at Baille Hill. The latter was the city gaol until 1880, situated on the opposite bank of the river, the castle being the county institution. It had for some time operated its own gallows and kept them exclusively for those whose crimes had taken place within the city walls.

The first of his duties, the hanging of Michael Shaw, had been undertaken without event. It was during his short journey to Baille Hill on the Castlegate ferry that the trouble began. John was recognised by the crowd, also on their way to the second of

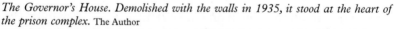

The Governor's House. Demolished with the walls in 1935, it stood at the heart of the prison complex. The Author

the day's morbid amusement. For reasons, never explained, they began to jeer and manhandle him, to such an extent that he arrived at the city gaol unable to continue without a stiff drink. The *Yorkshire Gazette* remarked... 'which a sterner and more relentless character would not have required.'

Taking his place upon the gallows platform it was obvious that the drink had affected him. Whilst fixing the rope to the beam his jocular manner hardly befitted the occasion. At one point he even shook the noose at the spectators and shouted, 'Some of you come up and I'll try it!' The whole scene became more incompetent with the arrival of the condemned man, William Brown, on the stage. John struggled to fit the hood over his head and then discovered that the rope was too short. No matter how hard he tried, the noose would not stay put around the man's neck. The crowd heckled and barracked, until finally it was left to the under-sheriff to complete the task in hand. On his return home, John was knocked down and beaten by an angry mob. Once again, the reporters of the *Gazette* were never afraid to pass an opinion:

We do not excuse the man's conduct; but it is due to the Sheriffs of this city, to justify their selection of the individual, and to the man himself to explain how the unfortunate occurrence arose.

Later that same year, while carrying out a multiple execution, he managed to fall through the platform as the bolt was removed and plummet with his victims. Much to the delight of the assembly, he re-appeared severely shocked and bruised.

'Mutton' Curry continued in his job until 1835, when he retired, not to a life of leisure but to the Thirsk Poor House, where he died in poverty in 1841.

The man who took over John's old position also came from the castle. James Coates, a convicted burglar, escaped seven years of transportation by taking up the post, but in 1840 he absconded from the prison. Nathaniel Howard, a coal porter by trade, hanged sixteen between 1840-53 and was followed by Thomas Askern from Maltby near Doncaster. Askern held the post until 1878 and it was his retirement that brought to an end the city of York elevating its 'Gallow-Birds' to the post of hangman.

The windows of the prison still retain their bars. The Author

On 15 May 1878, the Corporation finally called in the Newgate executioner, the celebrated son of Horncastle, the Master Craftsman – William Marwood of Lincolnshire.

Marwood considered himself a true professional. Those who had gone before him were mere hangmen; he was an executioner. His complex tables of calculations, comparing a man's weight to the length of rope needed, were in use long after his death. His first employment in the city was to hang Vincent Walker for a murder committed in Hull, but the day did not go well. Walker twitched on the rope for a full seven minutes before his death and Marwood left the town red-faced. The authorities must have wished for the return of bungling Thomas Askern.

Had the city taken up the suggestion of the *Gazette* in 1835, then York would have had another hangman after John Curry's retirement:

If we might recommend a successor, we would propose a petition to His Majesty craving the use of Jonathan Martin in this service, so that the notorious individual, already execrated by all honest and good men, may become the abhorrence also of all malefactors and dishonest persons, and thus must be held in universal detestation and loathing.

Jonathan Martin?

Chapter 3

Jonathan Martin
and the Art of Insane Arson
The Minster Fire: 1829

Why don't we let Jonathan Martin introduce himself?

I was born in the year 1782, in the Parish of Hexham, in Northumberland, of poor but honest parents, who in time put me apprentice to the Tanning business, during which time nothing occurred worthy of relating. In my 22nd year I removed to London, my mind being intent on travelling to Foreign Countries.

He would get his wish, because he allowed himself to be press ganged aboard an old slave trader, the *Enterprize*, then attached to the King's Navy. This information comes to us from the pages of his autobiography, *The Life of Jonathan Martin of Darlington, Tanner,* of which he once claimed to have sold 14,000 copies. Its stories of his time in the navy are perhaps no more unusual than those of any other young man caught up in war and, as many do in such situations, he turned to religion. Or rather, as he believed, religion turned to him, and it would be these apparent revelations that would eventually spell trouble.

Jonathan was not the only son of Fenwick and Isabella Martin to achieve fame. For a short period in the 1820s his younger brother, John, had threatened Joseph Turner's popularity with his apocalyptic landscapes, teaming with life and incident. These paintings would shortly be brought to mind again in York; only on this occasion they would be more real than anything John Martin could produce on canvas. Jonathan also fancied himself to be something of an artist and the third edition of his autobiography was 'considerably improved with engravings by the author.'

Prior to his arrival in the city, in the December of 1828, Jonathan had spent time in two lunatic asylums. His first

The minster's west front, from a drawing by Herbert Railton (late nineteenth century). Author's collection

internment in West Auckland, County Durham, came as a result of his wife reporting to the authorities that an angel had instructed her husband to shoot the Bishop of Oxford with a pistol. His second spell inside an asylum was two and a half years in the famous Newcastle institution at Gateshead. He managed to escape from there through the roof in 1821, a fact of which he was immensely proud, and so seven years later we find him in York searching out lodgings, accompanied by second wife, Maria.

He came to rest close to the Minster, at the home of William Law, a shoemaker in Oldsworth. Law had no reason to be unduly concerned with his new lodger. He noted that he seemed to be a very religious man, with much of his time spent reading the bible; whilst his days were taken with trying to sell his autobiographical pamphlets at six shillings a copy. He attended religious meetings with the Methodists and also the Ranters, an anti-puritanical society formed in the seventeenth century. On Sundays, he would join the congregation at Evensong in the Minster.

William Law might have viewed his lodger differently had he been aware of a letter found pinned to the door of the Minster, dated 27 December 1828:

I write to you, O Clergymen! To warn you to repent, and fly the wrath which will come upon you. I warn you to repent, the torch is already lighted, and the Sword of Justice hangs over you. Your churches and your Ministries will come tumbling about your ears. Repent O, you Clergymen! You who have brought grievous curses on the land! You whitened sepulchres; you will suffer in hell for what you are doing! The son of Bonaparte is preparing that for you, and will finish that work which his father left undone.
No. 2 Oldsworth, York. Jonathan Martin

The letter was ignored, as were others that were found fastened to the choir gates during January 1829. 'Your gret Charchis and Minstairs will cume rattling down upon your gilty heads,' warned one such missive and with hindsight it should have been acted upon, but the staff at the Minster saw all sorts of religious zealots and dissenters keen to make their voices heard and so Jonathan was permitted to go about his daily life. He became a familiar face around the church, but was seen as harmless. As William Law would later state, he was led by his dreams, one of which was the destruction of London, another that Napoleon's son would rule England. Clearly a mad man; innocuous, but undoubtedly mad. However, Jonathan did have an ultimate design in mind and at the end of January he began its execution.

He left his lodgings at Oldsworth on 27 January, telling

Jonathan Martin produced this drawing in prison prior to his removal to London. The poem reads – 'That's the Lord, I am the hand. That's the cloud that God command[s]. April 16th 1829.' The Wellcome Trust

William Law that he was bound for Leeds. But he had no intention of ever going there. He secured a room in Tadcaster and on the morning of Sunday, 1 February, Jonathan left his wife and returned to York. That night he attended Evensong at the Minster once more.

At some time during the service he left the congregation and hid behind Archbishop Greenfield's tomb in the north transept. There he remained until the clergy, choristers and vergers left at 6.30 pm, locking the door behind them. Free to work at will, Jonathan began the completion of his plan.

From the belfry tower he cut down twenty-seven meters of rope and using the skills gained at sea, knotted a ladder, which he used to scale the choir gates. His candlelight was seen by a passerby at 8.30 pm and by two prisoners in the Peter Prison west of the Minster at 9 pm, but neither gave it much attention. Meanwhile, inside, Jonathan was busy constructing a bonfire.

Kneeling cushions were ripped with a razor and piled up. Then he collected all the prayer books and anything else that would burn, making two piles either side of the choir. Happy with his work, he lit the pyres and watched them steadily take hold. At 3 am he dragged the window cleaners gantry to the north transept and using the rope ladder, left through a window into the Deanery garden.

The glare was seen an hour after Jonathan's departure, but the observer assumed that workmen were working through the night. Yet again, at 5 am, explosive volleys were heard from within the Minster and ignored. It was 7 am before the fire was discovered.

Master Robert Swinbank, junior chorister, arrived for early practice and finding the Minster locked, took to sliding about in the morning frost. He slipped, and once prone on his back, he could see smoke billowing from the west tower.

With the alarm finally raised, Job Knowles, the sexton, arrived close on the heels of a stonemason, Mr Scott. Entry through the south transept proved impossible, so they got in through the vestry. The fire had not at that time taken a firm hold, but the influx of fresh air as doors were opened soon caused it to strengthen. Clergy and volunteers tried to salvage what they could, but by 8 am the flames had engulfed the organ and the rescue of valuables proved dangerous. The Minster engine was

The Minster rises above Petergate. The Author

The Minster viewed from the north. The central tower is to the left. The Author

brought from the vestry and put to work in the south aisle, while the city engine was called and placed in the north aisle. Men of advancing years and infirmity, unfortunately, manned both; what's more no one seemed to be in charge. Confusion reigned as orders were barked from all quarters and this allowed the fire to grow unheeded.

Across the city, church bells rang out in alarm, bringing more volunteers and sightseers running to the blazing Minster. The Yorkshire Insurance Company engine was next on the scene and it proved as ineffective as the others. Not until the arrival of a company of Dragoon Guards, under the command of Major Clark, and Mr Bielby Thompson's fire crew from Escrick Park did any order ensue, but the dragoons work was hampered when their water supply became blocked with debris.

At 10.30 am the forty metre high roof collapsed into the choir below and it now seemed that the entire cathedral would be lost. In actual fact, it was this collapse that saved it.

More fire engines arrived from Leeds. The journey took nearly two hours and of the four dispatched, only one proved of immediate use. One was delayed by a broken wheel, another by the death of one of its horses, while the second engine to make the Minster overturned in its haste.

Efforts to subdue the fire went on until early evening and damping down of the smouldering wreckage was carried out through the night. The rope ladder that Jonathan had used to make his escape was found, along with a pair of shoemaker's pincers, stolen from William Law's. As thoughts turned to the person responsible for such an unholy crime, one name was on everyone's lips; that of Jonathan Martin. Now his letters seemed to make sense. Not just the wild ramblings of a mad man, but real threats carried out in devastating fashion.

With the aid of his former landlord, Maria Martin was located, but she was alone and could not believe what her husband was being accused of. A huge manhunt was set in place and, wanted posters, offering a reward of £100 were nailed around the city. Newspapers in the north carried the story of the fire and also of the need to capture the fugitive, describing him as a...

...rather stout man, about 5′ 6″ with light brown hair cut close, coming to a point in the centre of his forehead, with large bushy red whiskers.

Jonathan, meanwhile, had taken immediate flight. His first port of call was to the home of his former brother-in-law, Henry Carlton of Northallerton. He informed Carlton that he was making his way north to an uncle in Hexham. Having begged a night's board, he borrowed three shillings and sixpence and caught a ride on a coal wagon bound for Darlington. From there he proceeded on foot to the village of Codlaw Hill, eight kilometres north of Hexham. The family had moved to a cottage, not far from there, when Jonathan had been seven years old and the home of his distant relative, Edward Kell, had been then, as it was again, a refuge for the young boy with the troubled mind.

By 6 February the news of his crime was well known throughout the North of England. In Hexham, Sheriff's Officer, William Stainthorpe, soon learnt of a man answering the fugitive's description and upon confronting him with his identity found he was indeed Jonathan Martin. Taken to the gaol at Hexham, Jonathan was keen to know what people thought of him. Was he as famous as he supposed?

He was taken, in secret, back to York and placed in Peter Prison, within sight of his crime. On 9 February he admitted to

The Minster's west front looking from Duncombe Place, formerly Lop Lane and the site of Peter's Prison. The Author

the charge of arson and was taken to the city gaol at Baille Hill. Whilst there he attempted to escape up a chimneystack, but found his progress halted by iron bars. When questioned, he told the gaoler that God, who had told him to destroy the Minster, had now decided that he should suffer for it.

On 23 March, his trial opened at the Guildhall, used for crimes committed within the city, but his counsel argued that with a jury of local men a fair hearing could not be guaranteed. The case was then transferred to the county court and adjourned until 26 March. The esteemed Henry Brougham would head his defence team. Brougham was a leading advocate and Whig politician, whose circle of friends included many radical thinkers of the day. He had come to prominence in 1821 as the man who defended Queen Caroline of Brunswick during her famous defence of her marriage to King George the fourth. In supporting her, he had schemed to further the aims of the Whigs, a plan that failed. Within a year, he would be elevated to the position of Lord Chancellor in the government of Lord Grey, but however principled Brougham may have been, he did not come cheap and those costs were met by Jonathan's brother, John.

When Jonathan finally stood in the dock on 31 March, it was

not for his defence counsel to argue his innocence, as his guilt was never in doubt; it was his job to convince the jury that his client was of unsound mind. The jury, none of whom lived in the city, accepted this argument and after five minutes deliberation returned a verdict of 'guilty due to insanity'. Judge Bullock then informed the foreman that the correct wording of the verdict should be 'not guilty due insanity,' thereby saving Jonathan from a meeting with John Curry and his noose. The sentence handed out was that he should spend his life in the Criminal Lunatic Asylum at St George's Field in London, known to all by its more common name of Bedlam.

Before his removal in April to London, Charles Dickens made a visit to Jonathan in his cell at Baille Hill. He found him triumphant and lacking any remorse:

He was certain that all would work together for good – for his own good and for that of his country and of mankind. He was as vain of his exploits as if he had redeemed a race from slavery, or won the most glorious of victories.

His dissenting view of religion had been taken to its ultimate end and several physicians, having also visited him, branded him with the title of 'Religious Monomaniac.' But there was also an inflated perception of his own importance, the feeling that those high-living, wine drenched priests should have their punishment delivered from God by his own hand. His words to Dickens reveal much about how he viewed his place in the world:

I was nobody, and now more talked about than anybody. Who is there in the land who is not occupied with the name of Jonathan Martin? His name was known to nobody; it is now known to everybody. The King is now talking about me.... What is to happen? I maybe acquitted. What then? I shall know that I am

On 26 April 1829, Jonathan presented this drawing of himself in battle with the Black Lion to Caleb Williams, one the surgeons who pronounced him insane at his trial. It was given to the Dean and Chapter by Caleb's son, Isaac in 1890.
The Dean and Chapter of York.

preserved for, and appointed to, some greater work. God has yet something for me to do, and it will be done. Or they may find me guilty. They may be too blind to perceive the truth... .

Just before his death on 27 May 1838, Dickens visited him again. Jonathan spoke to him of Armageddon, of how he was due to bring about all the terrors contained within Revelations. Dickens asked that he be watched most carefully fearing that he was about to implement some outrageous act.

So this was the man whom the *Yorkshire Gazette* called upon to be the city executioner. Not surprisingly nobody took the suggestion further. The feeling in York for the man who tried to destroy the city's great symbol of the Anglican Church is best summed up by an inscription, scratched by a workman on a high window in the Minster:

Jonathan Martin on trial. The rope ladder, produced in evidence, hangs across the rails of the dock. Published 6 April 1829 by A. Barclay, Bookseller of York. Author's collection

York Minster burnt February 2nd 1829 by that damned Jonathan Martin. He ought to have been hanged, but anyhow he got right well damned by the citizens of York.

The church was of course repaired and rebuilt, unlike the life of a young man named Richard Martin. Richard was the son of Jonathan, born to his first wife in 1814. At fifteen years old, when his father had reached the height of his infamy, he was taken in by John Martin. For eight years he received the tutoring of his uncle, and was lucky enough to have inherited the Martin's artistic abilities. Two of his paintings were deemed good enough to hang in the Royal Academy. On Sunday, 5 August 1838, less than three months after his father's death in Bedlam and with his mind in turmoil, Richard took a razor to his throat and committed suicide.

Chapter 4

The Asylum

Bootham Park: 1838

In 1772, at a meeting of concerned citizens, it was decided that due to the 'deplorable condition of poor lunaticks in this extensive county, who have no other support than what a needy parent can bestow, or a thrifty parish officer provide', an asylum should be built, 'a public edifice for the reception of such unhappy people'. Modelled on those of Manchester and Newcastle, it would be a place of hospitalisation, not incarceration, going along with the new idea of the time that the insane could be cared for rather than brutalised.

For those suffering mental illness in the eighteenth century, treatment of any kind was a rare commodity. Many found themselves turned from their homes to wander the streets, eventually ending up in prisons and workhouses. Such institutions often set aside areas for 'lunatics' and 'idiots', leaving them to dissolve into worse conditions. Those families unable to undertake such drastic measures would be forced to lock their problems away in spare rooms, beneath the stairs or in outbuildings. Private madhouses existed for those with the means to pay, but having entered, their pecuniary value was so great that they rarely left.

Despite its founder's philanthropic ideals, the York Asylum would attract controversy during the early years. Designed by the prolific architect, John Carr, the asylum opened on a five-acre site, just off the Wiggington Road, on 1 November 1777. Intended for the treatment of 'the poor and the poor only,' its management soon contrived to fraud both patients and public.

The only physician employed, Dr Hunter, applied a mixture of obscure tonics and potions, whilst medical notes were lacking in any useful detail. At annual fund raising events, apparently cured individuals were brought forward to illustrate success, but behind the scenes, the hospital was being used to make money.

The John Carr designed York Lunatic Asylum, now Bootham Park Hospital. The Author

The Retreat. Its simple style contrast sharply with the Palladian design of the York Asylum. The Author

Affluent patients would be admitted and like the private madhouses, treatment would become protracted in the hope of securing additional charges. In 1790, suspicions were raised by a group of Quakers.

Hannah Mills was admitted to the asylum on 5 March. The Leeds Meeting wrote to their York Friends asking that they visit the unfortunate Hannah to comfort her and provide support. They were repeatedly refused admission and within a few weeks, Hannah died. At the suggestion of his daughter, Anne, and withstanding the objections of his fellow Quakers, William Tuke founded The Retreat in 1796. Still there today, it provided a basis for the treatment of mental illness throughout the world. The idea of a homely environment, supplying health care, recreation and employment to 'lunatics' was far ahead of its time. Indeed, so far ahead, that the governors of the city asylum bitterly resented its existence, and the barbed comments of its founders.

The governors of the York Asylum, seemingly unaware of the facts, were happy to point to the record of results as proof of success. The annual report of 1800 listed 1,347 patients admitted since opening. Of these, 655 had been cured, 307 relieved while 153 incurables were removed at the 'desire of friends.' There had been 120 deaths, but the all-important bank balance showed a healthy fund in excess of £3,000.

In 1804, Dr Hunter retired and Dr Best took up the position. He inherited the secrets of mixing purgatives with emetics, fortified with alcohol and opium; of douching, cupping and bleeding, all guaranteed to calm the frenzied mind. Cures were invented at will, because what mattered most was the control and pacification of the patients. A calm mind was open to reason and they brought about that state in whatever way they saw fit. It was a commonly held belief that lunatics became impervious to physical cruelty, leaving only their self-respect as a means of control.

The seeds of reform would once again be sown by the Tuke family.

In 1813, William Tuke's son, Samuel, published his book, *Description of The Retreat*. The asylum physician was angered by the suggestion within that The Retreat was born out of The

Asylum's neglect for Hannah Mills and he let Samuel know this. In reply, Samuel Tuke led a party of citizens in paying their £20 subscription, thereby securing seats on the board of governors of The Asylum. Having gained access to the records, their examinations revealed the inexcusable state of management.

For those patients capable of paying, the conditions were acceptable, but the poor, for whom the hospital had been founded, suffered terribly. The new governors, well acquainted with prisons and workhouses, reported that they had never seen such sights. Seven keepers looked after 199 patients and of these, 100 existed in filth without care or attention, locked wholesale in dark damp rooms to await scurrilous exploitation. A third of the 341 deaths had gone unrecorded, other than being a number and corruption was rife. Clearly, sweeping reforms were needed, but as more investigations got underway, disaster struck.

On 27 December 1813, a fire swept through the building, destroying evidence and killing four patients. During the blaze, one man escaped and his 'wanted notice' read like that of an escaped felon with its handsome reward on offer. Evidence of arson was lacking, but that did not stop people from speculating. However, it had come too late, and chaired by the Archbishop, the Governors found that one poor soul, Martha Kidd, had died as a result of gross neglect. It was all that was needed to instigate change in management and administration. Dr Baldwin Blake became the new physician, a man more in tune with new methods, and with a new board keen to see The Asylum succeed as a hospital rather than a source of income, things began to improve significantly. The whole episode led, in 1815, to a House of Commons Select Committee recommending a course of action that would improve the care for the mentally ill on a national scale. Godfrey Higgins JP, of Skellow Grange near Doncaster, gave his evidence before that committee on 1 May.

In 1813, he had sent William Vickers to the asylum following a case of assault. When the man returned home his family were shocked at the treatment he had received and let Higgins know of it. George Higgins made it his place to investigate and gained a seat on the board of governors alongside Samuel Tuke.

Though he had toured the hospital, Higgins always suspected that he had not been shown every room. So in the spring of 1814, he went early in the morning, determined to examine the whole building.

He ordered door after door to be unlocked until he reached the basement kitchens and came across a doorway he had not seen before. Higgins asked for it to be unlocked but the head keeper told him that the door led to the female apartments and he had no key. The suspicious magistrate threatened to open it himself with the aid of a large fireside poker, whereupon the key was miraculously located. Behind the door lay a narrow passageway, and off it, four dark cells, each about two metres square. The cells were furnished with nothing but damp straw and the air was thick with the stench of urine. Excrement covered the floors and walls, so thick that it filled the airbricks. Higgins asked who inhabited these noxious rooms and was informed that they were only used at night by a few women. He demanded to see the women and was led up a flight of stairs to another room, some three metres by two. In the room sat thirteen women, whose condition horrified Higgins, so much so that he was forced to leave and seek fresh air.

A meeting of the governors had already been called for 12.00 pm that day and when Higgins told them of what he had found, not one of them knew of the basement cells. While Higgins had been away, the rooms were cleaned but time had not allowed a decent job of it. The evidence was there for all to see and Higgins lifted the straw with the tip of his umbrella to reveal a chain and handcuffs bolted to the stone floor. Mr Atkinson, the apothecary, who accompanied the governors, admitted that he knew of the situation. There were wholesale dismissals, but many of the staff simply set up private institutions of their own. Stories emerged of female patients having had children to keepers, patients suffering extreme physical abuse and others who simply vanished, their families left to wonder what had happened to them. One of the original head keepers, James Backhouse, who received a silver plate on his retirement in 1803 for outstanding service and conduct, had in 1797, paid the Overseers of the Poor of the Parish of Louth, £30 in respect of a child he had fathered with former patient Elizabeth West.

Two tales of a very different nature come from the 1830s, from a time when reforms were well underway.

At 3 am, on the last Wednesday in July 1831, an unnamed patient wrenched free the bars of his window and made his escape. Having always wanted to visit Ripon, he made his way to the river, thinking that he could follow it to his desired destination. In theory, a journey of some twenty-nine kilometres and maybe he would have succeeded had he not headed downstream instead of up.

He arrived, of course, at the Archbishop's Palace in Bishopthorpe and entering the gardens 'enjoyed himself not a little.' From there, he crossed the hedge into Reverend Dixon's garden and eventually the churchyard. Seeing a ladder against the wall, he gained admission to the church and headed aloft to the belfry and upwards into the roof. Once there, he removed several slates to let in the light, allowing him to enjoy the view.

Having descended back to the pews, he fashioned an elaborate turban from a blue curtain and, collecting as many prayer books as he could carry, made his way back to the belfry. But this man was no Jonathan Martin, because he then began to sing aloud and in the process caught the bell with his foot. Liking the sound and eager to accompany his singing, our fugitive then began to strike the bell with enthusiastic vigour. His efforts woke the sexton, who hurried half dressed into the

The River Ouse as it passes the Palace at Bishopthorpe. The Author

The solitary ruins of St Andrews Church at Bishopthorpe. The Author

churchyard. Afraid to enter the church, he called out – 'Hello! Who is ringing those bells?' A few moments later, a turbaned head poked through the gap in the church roof and answered – 'Nobody! For there's only one bell.'

The Sexton hurried in fright to the village, to collect help against what he described as an 'outlandish creature with a blue horn growing out of his head.' When the villagers arrived, the bravest of them entered the church and climbed to the belfry. Instead of an outlandish creature, he found the escapee, who greeted him courteously and informed him that he had been out on a ramble in the hope of a pleasant ride home. De-turbaned, he was set upon a cart and conveyed back to York. His only

The entrance to Bishopthorpe Palace. The Author

complaint being, that he thought that one of his Grace's carriages should deliver him.

Despite the new ways in The Asylum, controversy reared its head again 1838, highlighting the need for further change.

In the New Year, Thomas Ward, 52, of Whitby entered The Asylum: a quiet man with a troubled mind, whose family sought his former sanity. Another patient, Frank Parker, knew differently. He knew that the authorities had placed Ward into the hospital to kill him. Having no one to confide in, he chose to keep quiet and bide his time.

Frank Parker had entered The Asylum in April 1837 and he spent the first two months restrained for his own safety. Eventually, he calmed down and was set free, but although staff believed that he was no threat to other patients, his hands were often fastened to prevent him hurting himself.

At 10 am on 11 March 1838, Parker was put into the exercise yard with eight others, one of whom was Thomas Ward. Both men had their hands fastened to their sides; Parker for reasons already stated and Ward to stop him from ripping his clothes. Whilst in the yard, the men should have been attended at all times, as petty arguments would often flare up between patients; not surprisingly, given their situation and constant close quarters. Nevertheless, this was not always the case and it was not the case on 11 March.

Before that day, there had been no angry words between Parker and Ward, indeed the two men always seemed to be in good humour when together. But Parker had not mentioned what he knew. Without warning, Parker knocked Ward to the floor and proceeded to savagely kick him until he bled from open fractures to his head. An asylum servant, Mr Bower, seeing the fracas from a window ran to fetch Keeper John Wilkinson, who found Ward, face down, seemingly dead. Frank Parker stood over him, his boots and trousers besmirched with blood.

'Do you see what you have done?' said Bower.

'Yes,' answered Parker, his voice cool and unfeeling. 'I have killed the old devil.'

It was then that Ward let out a groan. Realising that he was alive, all be it barely, Wilkinson and Bower carried him into an anteroom and called for the physician, Dr Ellis. Thomas Ward lived just long enough for Ellis to oversee his moment of death.

Frank Parker was without remorse. Asked if he was sorry, he replied that he could not say. Ward had 'bunched' him and he returned the push. It was a fair fight, only he was the strongest. In the night, even without guilt, ghosts visited the dreams of Frank Parker. He claimed to have heard the voice of Ward crying out in the night and feared that he was not dead. He created such a fuss, that Steward Joseph Hursley took him to see the body.

'Will you believe?' Hursley asked.

'I think he's dead now,' sneered Parker.

'You may look upon yourself as a murderer,' said Hursley. 'This poor man is dead.'

'I am glad of it.' Parker answered. 'I wish to give myself up to justice. I have been here unlawfully detained and I should prefer the castle to this place.'

At his trial, he told the court of his fear that Ward was there in the asylum to kill him and so he 'got in first.' Found guilty of murder, he hung his head in shame and repeated his request for a cell in the castle. It was, he told the courtroom, the place where he belonged; adding that he would not have committed the crime had he been there from the start. Frank Parker got his wish. As the law did not allow an insane man to hang and unable to return to the asylum, he ended his days forgotten in York Castle.

A daunting façade. The Asylum entrance. The Author

Chapter 5

A Child Called Hannah

Acomb: 1839

In the summer of 1837, a young woman of about twenty-two years of age gave birth to a baby girl. For most, a time of happiness, but for Jane Norton it meant nothing but trouble. She was unmarried and living in the Pocklington Workhouse. Jane did not need a baby to care for, much less an illegitimate one with all the stigma that it carried. She cared so little for the girl that she left her without a name and placed her in the care of the Pocklington Poor Union.

The baby passed from house to house among the trustees, still nameless. For a short period she even lived with her maternal grandmother in Stamford Bridge, but for two and a half years, she remained Jane Norton's baby girl, with no name of her own. Then in early December 1839, Anne Snell of Newton upon Derwent took in the Norton child, and she called her Hannah.

Once Jane had dealt with her unwanted child, she left the Pocklington area and took a servants position at a house in Upper Poppleton. There, she met fellow servant Charles Gowland and they married at Bishophill Church on 11

The village green, Upper Poppleton. The Author

St Mary's Church in Bishophill Junior. The Author

November 1839. She kept no secrets from her new husband, he knew all about the illegitimate baby and together they visited her while she was with her grandmother. Nevertheless, Charles was clear about one thing; the girl would never live with them. He planned for a family of his own, and this did not include the offspring of his wife's previous imprudence.

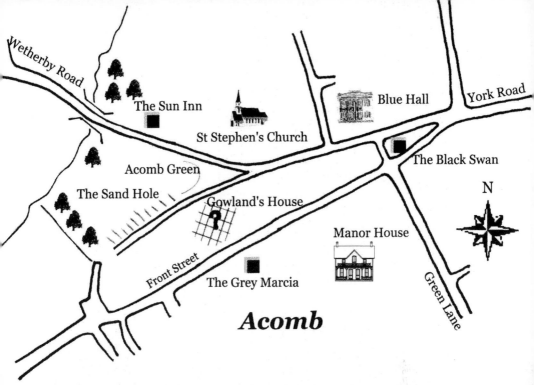

Acomb circa 1839. The Author

After the wedding, the Gowlands took a house in the village of Acomb, in a yard on top of the hill, overlooking the Sandhole (now Acomb Green). Acomb at this time was far from the sprawling suburbia of today and it provided an ideal base for Charles's new employment as a navigator on the expanding railway system. Although the marriage was new, it was not the happiest. Jane continually neglected to pay the local traders for goods, particularly milk and beer, and Charles was always answering the door to shopkeepers pursuing payment.

Meanwhile, word of Jane Norton's marriage reached the trustees of the Pocklington Union and they decided to re-unite mother and daughter. Anne Snell, the one person who cared enough to name the little girl, had her in her care for only two weeks, when John Jackson and Thomas Brown took Hannah

Acomb Green, known in the nineteenth century as The Sandhole. The Author

away and set out for Acomb on 20 December 1839.

They arrived in the village at around 10 am and entered the *Black Swan*, both to warm themselves and ask directions to the Gowland's house. Unbeknown to them, a figure watched their entrance with surprised interest. Charles Gowland was drinking with friends at the bar and recognised the shivering child at once.

The pub was doing a brisk trade and Jackson set Hannah by the fire, while the two men ordered drinks and asked after Jane Gowland. The landlord, William Wood, informed them that they were in luck, as her husband was in the room, but Charles Gowland had left. He knew what was afoot and dashed home to let Jane know that the trustees were trying to bring her daughter. He made his feelings clear, before heading back to the pub.

During the time he had been away, his friends, Pat Curry and John Richardson, had been keeping company with the trustees and Hannah. Charles was not pleased to see the group sat together around the fire, and much less to be pointed out to John Jackson as being the man he sought. Jackson told him of their purpose, but Charles left him in no doubt as to what would happen if they burdened him with the child – he would desert his wife, leaving her penniless and once again subject to the benevolence of the poor union.

John Jackson was not a man easily deferred from his task, indeed, at the meeting of the Pocklington Union it had been he who had insisted on returning Hannah to her mother. Alone, he went to the Gowland house and told Jane that he intended to bring her daughter. He hoped, he told her, that she and the girl could live together in happiness with Charles Gowland. Jane repeated what her husband had told both of them; that he would leave. What's more, she claimed to be pregnant and unable to provide for two children.

Jackson returned to the *Black Swan*, determined to finish what he came to do. Charles Gowland had left with his friends and so Jackson and Brown carried Hannah to her mother. Despite her protests, they gave her no choice and mother and daughter were finally reunited.

Charles and his drinking companions went into York. They visited several alehouses and rolled into *The Black Boy* on North Street sometime after midday. Also in the pub that afternoon

Looking up the hill at Acomb. The Author

was Hester Skelton from Knapton, a former colleague of the Gowlands from their domestic service days in Upper Poppleton. She latched onto the party and around 5 pm they returned to Acomb. The four of them found Jane Gowland sat on a box in tears. Charles took her to one side and for two minutes, they whispered to one another. He discovered that the trustees had delivered the child despite his warning, but that she had turned them away.

Hester had already been told something of what was happening and told Charles in no uncertain terms what she thought. He had known about Jane's baby before he had married, and so must accept her. She took Jane into another room, in an effort to console her and asked if she had seen the girl. Jane told her that she had not, that the child had remained in the *Black Swan*.

'I don't wish to see it,' she said. 'I hate it!'

Hester Skelton remained with the Gowlands for a little over two weeks. During that time, she saw Jane regularly burst into tears, but nothing made her overly concerned.

The next six months passed without event. The trustees of the Pocklington Union were happy to have returned Hannah Norton to her mother. Charles Gowland went about his business in the reassuring knowledge that his wife had been strong enough to turn her illegitimate brat away. His spendthrift wife, whiled away the weeks not daring to answer the door and sobbing in quiet moments.

Then, at the start of June 1840, they vanished.

The little house stood empty for about a week, until landlord Charles Robinson, gave up for lost his rent and let the rooms again. Before the new couple took up residence, he employed another tenant of his, Elizabeth Barton, to clean the house. She noticed something strange. Many of the wooden fixtures in the house had been removed. Elizabeth was no fool, she knew that it was an old trick for tenants unable to buy coal to burn the fittings, but the Gowlands coal house held a plentiful supply. She dismissed it from her mind; who knew what daft things folk got up to and after all, it was no concern of hers. Neither did she take much notice of close neighbours who complained of a nauseating smell emanating from the house. Elizabeth Barton could smell nothing.

Chapel Terrace stands up the hill in Acomb. The Author

The new tenants moved in a few days later. Thomas Metcalf and his wife Eliza could smell something straight away, but a good search of the property revealed nothing obvious. Eliza Metcalf felt that the sickly stench was strongest on the staircase and so she inspected the coal store beneath it, reached by an outside door. Perhaps a cat had ventured in and been trapped, or possibly a rat had been poisoned and crawled in to die. Having moved some coals she could see a ragged bundle at the back of the store. Unable to reach it, she fetched her husband.

Thomas Metcalf brought a rake and dragged the bundle forward. In spite of being decayed and crawling with maggots, it was clearly a little girl. Neighbours soon realised that it must be Hannah Norton.

A postmortem was undertaken in a barn at the rear of the *Grey Marcia* public house by local surgeon, Dr Brydges Hodgson. He presented his findings the next day at the inquest.

The child had met with a violent death. A heavy weapon had been used to damage the girl's skull and some teeth had been broken. Several bruises were evident on the body and a strip of petticoat was still tightly pulled around her neck. The fact that the corpse had been locked in the store and covered in coals had lessened the rate of decomposition. Dr Hodgson, therefore, estimated death to have taken place a number of months ago.

The acting coroner, Matthew Pearson of Selby, was of the opinion that Hannah Norton met her violent end on that December afternoon. The question was by whom – Jane or Charles Gowland. Hester Skelton had not seen Hannah during her stay and Jane had told her that she had never been there. The

The Poacher, *formerly* The Gray Marcia. The Author

consensus was that Jane Gowland, fearful of her husband carrying out his threat to leave, murdered her daughter. Whatever she had whispered to Charles when he had returned home that night, the coroner thought that it was not to tell him of her deed. He found it inconceivable that Charles Gowland would have lived in the house for six months knowing the secret of the coal store without removing the body. It does beg the question why he was using the wooden fittings in the house to stoke the fire, but that particular subject was never fully addressed.

The jury concurred, and in her absence, found 'the wife of Charles Gowland guilty of the murder of Hannah Norton, her own daughter.'

It was said that the Gowlands were spotted on the road at Boroughbridge, or perhaps near Shipton. Either way, they had gone, leaving Hannah behind as Charles always said he would.

The old barn at the rear of the Gray Marcia, scene of Hannah's post-mortem examination. The Author

Chapter 6

The Horsefair Murder

Kings Staithe: 1853

The York Horse Show, held in the last full week before Christmas, was, for many years, one of the most important dates in the city's calendar. Breeders and dealers from across the north would descend upon the town and every inn's stables would quickly fill, indeed, much of the trading was done in the landlord's yard with the horses never reaching the fairground on the Wigginton Road. It became the most celebrated sale of horseflesh in the country.

In 1836, the King of Denmark purchased fifteen two year old coaching stallions at a price exceeding £200 each; an exorbitant sum of money. The year before, Don Carlos of Spain bought countless inferior grade horses, much to the delight of the Yorkshire breeders. The British Army was also a regular buyer and their contractors were more than well received.

The success of the show was boosted in the 1830s by the apparent fear in the South of the new railroads. Many of the southern breeders pulled out of the trade sure that the demand for a coaching horse would plummet. Initially, that fear proved to be unfounded and with good horses in short supply, the dealers headed north to fulfill their orders.

Of course, such an event attracted more than its fair share of shady characters and dodgy dealings.

Mr Taylor, a tobacconist of Bridge Street, was most surprised one Sunday morning to wake and find a Hackney pony standing at his front door. He was even more surprised to discover that the animal was the very same one that had been stolen from him three years previously off the Knavesmire. Mr Taylor's front door had at that time been the entrance to the Hackney's stable before conversion to a cottage. It soon transpired that a Nottinghamshire gentleman staying at the *Windmill Inn* had purchased the pony some time ago. Having taken him from the stable at the inn to groom him for sale, the pony slipped his halter and made for home; where, as the newspapers of the day recorded, he would be remaining – and legally so.

A popular trick among the 'sharpers' around the town was the 'blank paper scam' and though the press reported on it regularly, many a drunken fool fell for it.

The tricksters would first choose and befriend a well-heeled victim, making sure that the drink kept flowing. Having ensured the unfortunate man's trust they would make great play as to the safety of his money, telling him that it should be well wrapped so as to avoid pickpockets. By now the victim is well and truly inebriated and hands his money over so that his newfound friends can carry the task out for him. Only later, while nursing a hangover, will he discover that his tightly wrapped money roll is nothing but worthless sheets of blank paper.

Another trick required a degree of gullibility and greed on the part of the victim. The 'sharper' would turn out his *regular bad-un* (as the dealers called a poor horse) well groomed so as to disguise its faults. He would then approach an owner of a good horse and offer to make a swap. The owner of the fine animal would of course decline, stating the expected sale value of his steed. The 'sharper', though disappointed, politely accepts the refusal, but his accomplice is ready with the sting. He approaches the 'sharper' within earshot of the gentleman and offers a substantial sum for the inferior horse, which the 'sharper' turns down. Greed being a powerful inducement, the gentleman then changes his mind and takes up the offer of the swap. Even if he is lucky enough to find the accomplice, the gentleman will discover that the sale is no longer available and he is now the proud owner of a *regular bad-un.*

In 1853, the show is still going strong, and although the rail system is rapidly expanding (York being joined in 1839) and the heyday of coaching has gone, the horse is still the chosen transport for everyday life. One visitor to the fair is Mr John Hall of *Snainton New Inn*, between Malton and Scarborough.

John Hall was visiting the fair with his son. The purpose of their visit was business, but after disposing of a horse they were availing themselves of the hospitality of the city's numerous alehouses. The son returned home at about 3.30 pm, leaving his father in the smoking room of the *White Swan*, a well known

Pavement. York's busy coaching route still bustles with life. The Author

coaching inn on the Pavement. Robert Reed, the landlord, kept him well supplied, so much so, that when he left at 5.30 pm he was much the worse for liquor. He intended to make his way to *Barker's Hotel*, near the railway station, to see some friends and conduct some more business - but he never made it.

As well as the tricksters, pickpockets and thieves, such an influx of people and money to the city attracted another group of rogues – the prostitutes. The itinerants who followed the fairs and races about the North Country would swell York's already healthy population of street girls.

One of these traveling girls, Isabella Campbell, had lately come down from Berwick-upon-Tweed and hooked up with Caroline Nicholson who had a room in Middle Water Lane. They were of a similar age, about nineteen, and were both described as 'resembling the lower and more degrading class of street walker.'

The three Water Lanes, namely, First (demolished in 1851 and rebuilt as King Street), Middle (now Cumberland Street) and Far, ran downhill from Castlegate to the River Ouse. The building of Clifford Street in 1881 saw them swept away in a rush of Victorian development and Friargate is all that remains of Far Water Lane. They were dark, gothic, overcrowded tenements; wooden buildings that housed the desperate and the low. In the cholera epidemic of 1831, over ten per cent of all those who died lived in the Water Lanes. Many of the inhabitants gained a living on the wrong side of the law, forced by circumstance into thieving and prostitution. Along with Walmgate, the Irish came into the Water Lane district in the 1840s to work in the chicory industry. As an observer of the time noted, 'They were packed like herrings in boxes.' The census of 1851 lists among the wheelwrights and sailmakers, numerable paupers, beggars and hawkers. Isabella and Caroline would have been no shrinking violets, hardened to a life of filth and poverty.

On that festive December evening the girls were keeping an eye out for likely customers on the corner of Nessgate. At around 5.45 pm they spied a gentleman approaching. Dressed in a dark topcoat, a horse sheet rolled beneath his arm and obviously under the severe effect of alcohol, came publican John Hall.

The girls accosted him, one either side, and led him down King Street onto the Staith, where the barges and boats unloaded their goods. Caroline Nicholson wanted Hall to follow them to her house in Middle Water Lane, but he was not happy to do so. From that point on the girl's attitude changed. Several witnesses saw them pushing him around and he was in no fit state to put up a fight. One witness, Joseph Sargent, a rag-dealer from the Water Lanes, shouted out – 'Let the poor man alone,' but the girls laughed at him and carried on. As they pulled at his overcoat trying to find his purse, John Hall edged closer to the waters edge. In his drunken condition and with his back to it, he may not have realised that the river was even there. At this point, Isabella Campbell made a frantic grab inside his coat for the money.

'You'll not have it,' said Hall.

'Well have this then,' replied Campbell and with the slightest of touches sent him into the river. He could be seen for a fleeting moment before being sucked under the keel of a boat and away in the swollen winter waters.

A young lad by the name of 'Tot' grabbed a pole from a boat and plunged it into the water without success. He later claimed that he would not recognise either woman again and what's more, in his view the man was so drunk that he fell in the river having barely been touched. Another boy, Daniel Collins, claimed to have heard Caroline Nicholson say, 'Push him in, the bastard,' prior to Campbell doing just that.

In the ensuing calamity, Isabella and Caroline made a swift exit up the steps onto the Ouse Bridge and turned right towards Nessgate.

Unaware of what had happened, police officer William Catton was walking towards the bridge when the girls passed him at some speed. He had known Caroline Nicholson for five years since she started walking the streets and Isabella Campbell's character had come to his attention, so he turned and watched them enter *McGregor's Dram Shop* on Low Ousegate before continuing on his way. As he approached Ouse Bridge, he could hear the uproar and a crowd had gathered, encouraged by the cry of murder. From below, he could hear shouts of 'Take hold of it' and 'Hold it fast.' Running down the steps, Catton

King Street, formerly First Water Lane. The Author

was immediately grabbed by Joseph Sargent, who having quickly told him the tale, explained that he could identify the two girls.

They found them with some of their colleagues on the corner of Nessgate, no doubt having strengthened themselves with a drop of gin. 'Them's the two women,' said Sargent, and facing Isabella Campbell, 'That's the woman that pushed the man in the water.'

Officer Catton arrested them and when asking for the reason, and being told, Isabella said in disbelief, 'What me? Oh my goodness, I've never been on the Staith tonight.'

However, Catton knew them too well and led them down to the station. When searched by Margaret Whitwell, an officer's wife, a purse was found on Isabella Campbell - 'I wish I had stopped in the house; this would not have happened,' she moaned.

Taken in 1853, this photogrpah shows the King's Staithe in the year of John Hall's murder. A group of people can be seen on the dockside by the Ouse Bridge Inn *(now the* King's Arms*) at the very point where John Hall met his watery end.* York City Libraries

'Hold your noise.' snapped Caroline. 'They'll have something to do to find out.'

John Hall's body was fished out of the Ouse one hundred and thirty seven metres downstream at 8 pm, close to the public washing area, known as the 'Pudding Holes.' He was taken to the nearby *Jolly Sailor* public house and a local surgeon, Mr Crummack, was called, but Hall was quite dead. A search of his pockets revealed his money roll, some £50, still intact.

The next day, the girls stood in front of the magistrates at the Guildhall to hear that they would be remanded in the House of Correction at Toft's Green. On the following day, a coroner's inquest was held in the *Jolly Sailor* and after hearing witnesses statements, Coroner J P Wood gave the jury two options. If they thought that the girls had willfully pushed John Hall into the river, while trying to rob him, then that amounted to murder, however, if they were of the mind that they had pushed him in while attempting to cajole him into visiting their house – an act that they had no business to do – then the crime would be manslaughter. After an absence of one hour the jury returned a verdict of wilful murder.

Chapter 7

Unhappy Families

Paver Lane, Walmgate: 1856

It is very easy to become sentimental when speaking of the Victorian working class family. The image of the wife sat by her black cooking range, a wholesome meal simmering on the open fire, her doorstep pumiced clean, over which her hardworking husband will step to throw his cap on the hearth, is a cosy one.

Paver Lane is now little more than a non-descript connection between Walmgate and Percy Lane, but once it teemed with life. Families lived close to one another – tightly knit groups of powder kegs waiting for that igniting spark. The Fowler family were a typical Victorian working class family.

'Old (William) Fowler' lived with his wife, Jane, in Paver Lane. He was a general dealer, in other words he bought and sold what came his way. As a father, many thought him a grand chap; not many had a wrong word for him, partly due to pity. His wife, according to neighbours was a 'queer sort of woman at any time.' One minute she was friendly, the next she became argumentative and perhaps 'not right in the head,' because she talked to herself – not just the odd word, but for hours on end. Of course, the drink did not help – and not just the odd tipple, Jane could keep at it all day if the mood took her; which it often did.

The Fowlers had a daughter, also by the name of Jane. The neighbours had an opinion of her too – 'ignorant and very simple-minded... as simple as a child.' She spent much of her time with her mother, drinking and chatting, drinking and arguing, although she was married with a home of her own in Paver Lane. Her husband, Thomas Rylatt, worked both in the brickyards at Briscombe and Young, and for the Gas Works. He seems to have endured his wife's ways, which was odd, because there was also a six-month-old baby to consider.

On Saturday, 2 March 1856, Thomas Rylett arrived home

Paver Lane, before demolition. York City Archives

from the brickyard at 6 pm and finding his own house empty, made for that of his in-laws. Mother and daughter sat by the fire, where a large pan of potatoes boiled for supper. It was obvious that they had both been at the ale, but they were not at that time completely drunk. Jane Fowler went out to the *Bricklayer's Arms* to fetch 'Old Fowler', because supper was ready and she was not going to let him miss it, not after he complained that she had not been feeding him properly of late.

While her mother was away, Jane Rylett told her husband that she had been arguing with her mother during the day, although things were right between them now. Thomas did not take a lot of notice; it was the same old story. At 11 pm, he left for the night shift at the gas works. At the same time, 'Old Fowler' retired to his bed. The two Janes remained downstairs to continue their drinking. The bottle ran dry at 1 am Sunday morning and Jane then decided to go home. She had not gone far when she realised that she had lost her door key.

With a sober mind, she would have turned and retraced her steps to her parent's house, but Jane was not sober. She was on her way home having left her baby in the care of her inebriated mother. She called at the neighbouring home of Alice Quinn, who was in the company of a young girl by the name of Elizabeth Othick and asked if they could help. The women noticed her drunken condition.

'Aye my lass,' confirmed Jane. 'I've had two or three pennorths.'

They accompanied her to her house to see if she had left the key in the door. She had not, and so Jane asked Elizabeth to go with her to her mother's.

'The old woman will have it,' she laughed.

Elizabeth Othick knew all about Jane Fowler. She had no desire to witness her sharp tongue and foul temper, so she agreed to go as far as the door and wait while the key was found. This she did, standing in the street for ten minutes, at which point she found it necessary to try and open the door.

'Hello! Who's there?' came Jane Fowler's cry.

'Only me, a woman,' replied Elizabeth.

'Open the door, mother,' called Jane Rylett. 'It's a young person who's been at Mrs Quinn's.'

Jane Fowler greeted Elizabeth with a knife in her hand. She had been frying some meat on the fire, beside which sat Jane Rylett, baby at her breast. No sooner had Elizabeth crossed the threshold, than Jane Fowler began the abuse. Cursing and shouting, she threatened to strike her with the poker. Elizabeth stood her ground, but when old Jane made to pick the poker up, young Jane pulled at her skirts and beckoned in earnest towards the door.

Hearing the door locked behind her, Elizabeth pressed her ear to it and listened. She heard Jane Rylett scream – 'Oh mother, mother don't,' followed by her mother calling for Jane's father – 'Oh Fowler, Fowler! Come down at once.' Elizabeth held her breath and waited, but it was quiet. Then she heard the sound of someone coming to the door and quickly she walked away. As she reached Alice Quinn's house, 'Old Fowler' appeared in his nightshirt.

The chimney of the York Gas Works, towers above neighbouring gardens..
Author's collection

'Is Thomas up?' he cried, meaning Alice's husband. Elizabeth nodded. 'He's to come at once, for Jane is pouring in blood,' said 'Old Fowler'.

Elizabeth was going to complain about her treatment at the hands of his cantankerous wife, but he had dashed straight back home. Alice Quinn was none too keen for Thomas to go, fearing that he too would fall foul of Jane Fowler's temper. Thomas, not being one to upset his wife, particularly at that time in the morning, stayed in his bed. The time was 2 am.

Old Fowler found his daughter where he had left her, lying by the coalhole door in the kitchen. She was bleeding from the neck and there was so much blood the wound was not visible. His wife told him that Jane had slipped from the stool and banged her head. When Thomas Quinn failed to arrive, Old Fowler called for no one else. He wrapped some cloths around his daughter's neck and carried her to bed, where she lay bleeding.

Thomas Rylett arrived home from the gas works at 8 am to the news that his wife was ill. They did not tell him what she was ill with, and so Thomas entered the bedroom possibly expecting a bout of flu or the after effects of alcohol.

Jane lay pale and still. The bleeding had stopped and the crude bandages replaced with a sticking plaster. Thomas asked her what had happened, but Jane would not say. He could see that she had been bleeding; yet he did not seem alarmed. Jane complained of a headache and could not bear to be moved. When Thomas lifted her head to help her drink a cup of tea, the pain was unbearable. He stayed by her side until 11 am, when she fell asleep and he went home to his own bed.

At around 1 pm, Thomas returned to the Fowlers for lunch. He sat around the table with Jane and Old Fowler without the conversation dwelling too long on the plight of his wife. His mother-in-law told him that Jane had woken briefly and taken some broth. She was now asleep again, although feeling much better. With lunch at an end, Thomas, happy to learn of his wife's improvement, retired once more to a bed in the house. Old Fowler, who explained to him that he had been awake all night, joined him on this occasion.

However, Jane was not feeling better; she was in fact dying. At 3 pm, she woke the house with a bout of violent coughing. This

Modern day Paver Lane. The building on the right is an old coaching shed, the only survivor of slum appearance. The Author

started the wound to bleed once more and only now did anyone think to call for help - not though, for a doctor, but for Mrs Blain, landlady of the *Bricklayer's Arms*. She saw straight away what the family had not. Immediately she ordered Old Fowler to fetch someone. Jane started to vomit and when Mrs Blain lifted the poor girls head to drink, she saw her hands covered in blood. The wound now visible, spouted like a fountain. Calling for some cloths, she attempted to stem the flow, without success.

Old Fowler then returned, alone, without any help.

'Oh do fetch someone,' cried Mrs Blain. 'Or there will be two of us dead in the room together.'

Swiftly, he departed once more and came back, not with a doctor, but with another neighbour, Mrs Hardcastle. It was all too little, too late. With a rattle in her throat, Jane Rylett breathed her last and died. Her mother collapsed, screaming and weeping. Her daughter, she sobbed, had banged her head on the coalhole door, or the spout of the kettle, or the poker, or... the story changed so often.

When Doctor Edward Allen finally attended, he was certain that the wound could only have been caused by a sharp instrument: a knife for instance. The force used to inflict the wound had been considerable, the carotid artery being punctured. Jane Rylett had bled to death and the bed on which she lay was steeped in the evidence.

The inquest, under the coroner, Mr J P Wood, was held in the *Bricklayer's Arms*. Having heard the evidence, Mr Wood instructed the jury as to its choice of decisions. If they thought

Walmgate Bar, for years the traditional home of the local police constable. The Author

Dennis Street, of Walmgate, escaped demolition and is typical of the better quality Victorian workers' housing. The Author

it probable, even possible, that Jane Rylett received her injury by falling from a stool, the verdict was accidental death. If, on the other hand, they believed another had inflicted the wound, it was down to them to decide who that person was. Having made that judgment, it was their duty to consider whether the deed was manslaughter or murder.

This was not as clear-cut as it might sound. Not, at least, in the view of the coroner.

Had the mother lashed out with a deadly weapon when only angry words were spoken, then it was murder. However, had she been provoked and hit out with a stick or fist, the verdict was manslaughter. Jane Fowler, though, had lashed out with a knife – murder then. But murder required malice aforethought and no evidence had been brought forward to suggest that.

This difficult conundrum took the jury no more than a few minutes of deliberation. In their eyes, Jane Fowler had been provoked (despite a clear lack of proof) and so the verdict was 'manslaughter against the mother of the deceased.' With less than a week to the next assizes, Mr Wood bound over the witnesses to appear and called for the arrest of Jane Fowler. At that moment, a messenger entered the room and called out for Dr Allen. He was to come quickly to the Fowler house as Jane Fowler was dying. They did not, on this occasion, call for Thomas Quinn, Mrs Blain or Mrs Hardcastle to provide medical attention.

Dr Allen found that the old woman was not dying, merely gripped by a fit of hysterics. He affected an instant cure by telling her that the verdict was manslaughter, not murder.

Chapter 8

A Policeman's Lot

Parish Constable Cowton: 1857
– and other constabulary tales

Y ork was no different to other provincial towns, in that, at first, it did not wholeheartedly embrace the introduction of Peel's New Police, following the formation of the Metropolitan Force in 1829. The authorities saw no reason for justice to be handed over to a seemingly military organisation and so it stuck with its watchmen.

The system of watchmen had been introduced to the city in 1774 and viewed by its founders, and the press, with much pride. However, it was the condemnation of these very watchmen and their conduct that brought about change in the way the streets were policed. Many argued that they were little better than the criminals they were employed to apprehend. They were easily led, easily bribed and overly fond of a

The very first police station was sited here on Silver Street. The Author

comfortable chair by an inn fire, often in dubious company. The low wage meant that many were forced to subsidise their income, and they were well placed to take advantage of illicit opportunities.

It was 1835 before York had its own police force. Following the *Municipal Boroughs Act* of the same year, intended to extend the Metropolitan blue print into the regions and the *Municipal Corporations Reform Act*, which reorganized the way in which the city was governed, a superintendent from London was employed. The Corporation recruited among the agricultural labourers; fit, healthy and strong-armed, used to working long hours in all weathers. If the man was unmarried, then all the better, as he was manageable and pliable. Once trained, his later marriage would hopefully provide the stability needed for this new upstanding member of the community. Not that the criminal fraternity viewed him with any great respect, indeed his uniform made him an easy target and the working classes saw him as an instrument of the bureaucracy. The job of policing York's streets was no easier for a member of the force in those early years than it is now.

On 11 May 1835, policeman Carter was set upon by four men and given a severe beating, leaving him a 'dreadful picture of brutality.' The men were never identified and no motive given, other than he was a policeman.

Later that same year, on 7 December, Captain Smith answered a cry of murder in Fossgate. A man came running towards him in a terrible state, telling of how he had been attacked by ruffians. Captain Smith, dedicated and keen, deputised a passer-by, Andrew Johnson, and together they took off over the Foss Bridge into Walmgate. It was clear from the noise emanating from Jackson's Yard that trouble was afoot. Smith entered, intent on dealing with the situation and found a fight taking place between two groups of men. He bravely attempted to quell the disturbance and arrest the ringleaders, but unfortunately, this caused the ruffians to join sides and set upon Smith and his civilian deputy. They were both knocked to the ground and repeatedly kicked. Smith's shoulder was dislocated and it was February before he returned to work.

The men employed by the Watch Committee of York rarely

Jackson's Yard, Walmgate. York City Archives

stayed long in the job. Their status in society was little better than a hotel porter and once trained, they often left to take up similar positions. Countless hours pounding the beat in a heavy uniform, took its toll on the healthiest of men and they lived among the very people whose trust they could not gain.

The process of improvement was slow and a meeting of the Watch Committee in July 1855 shows the mistrust that was building between the citizens and its policemen.

In general, it was felt that the conduct of the officers had been good and that there had been a number of improvements in efficiency but some areas caused concern, not surprisingly one of these was money. The cost of policing York had doubled since 1850, rising from £900 a year to more than £2,000. Never, said local farmer, Mr Charlton, had such a sum been wasted as it had on the police force. Chief Constable Robert Chalk, he continued, already overpaid was allowed £8 a year for clothing and yet he wore no livery, and what is more he had the audacity to keep a couple of cows near Mr Charlton's own pasture. This final statement raised laughter in the meeting, as those present knew that Charlton had reached his main source of disagreement.

Charlton had a recommendation to make to the committee. In his view, it was abundantly clear that Chalk was incapable of managing the city's twenty-eight full-time policemen. It was obvious that the positions of Superintendent of Police, Superintendent of the Scavenging Department and Inspector of Nuisances was too much for one man to undertake. The departments should be divided and an advertisement taken out asking for suitable applicants.

The committee took this outburst as a slight upon themselves and pointed out that they had nearly lost Chief Constable Chalk two years before upon a question of salary. It was unlikely that a man of his calibre could be replaced more cheaply.

Charlton's accusations produced an anonymous letter to the *Yorkshire Gazette* on 25 August 1855. Signed only 'a County Police Superintendent,' it leapt to Robert Chalk's defence and contained the following observations:

> ...*there is a rigidity of useless discipline enforced, which free men will not tolerate...the very system which lost us an army in Crimea deprives us of an efficient police force in York. The men are treated as automatons or mere machines – they are not allowed to have minds of their own... In York you are too much in the Metropolitan School, which is wholly unadapted to the provinces. Further, I would say give your Superintendent of Police a salary which will secure the entire services of an efficient man; and don't eke it out by converting him into an Inspector of Nuisances and a Captain of Scavengers.*

It could almost have been written by Chalk himself.

This frugality in funding the police came in for government criticism in 1856, but change was slow. It was felt by many that such a moralistic and religious community as York, could not require a large police force. To increase man power and spending would be to admit otherwise. But matters other than money troubled the good citizens, namely the state of certain areas of the city, and in particular, the Bedern.

Mr March made it known that the situation in that part of town had reached a disorderly state. During one Sunday in July 1855, while the good people of the town were walking to church, they were disturbed by a group of at least 150 people gathered at the Goodramgate end of Bedern. A fight broke out and yet not one policeman could be found. The Watch Committee claimed that they were all engaged at a situation in Micklegate. Nonsense, said Mr March, because he had been in that area on Sunday and though there was a surfeit of drunkards, he saw no policeman.

'Bedern' means 'House of Prayer'. The chapel is sited by the narrow entry to Goodramgate. The Author

Bedern, the former home of the College of Vicars Choral of the Minster, had degenerated through the early nineteenth century, until it had become a maze of tenements, dark and overrun. In the 1850s, the job of policing the area fell to one man, former workhouse inmate, Parish Constable Matthew Cowton. His story illustrates better than any other does the problem of keeping law and order in Victorian York.

Forty-two year old Cowton lived in the Bedern with his wife and six children. He joined the police sometime in 1852 and soon upset the large Irish population with his ways. In 1853, he arrested a young Irish lad for playing ball on a Sunday, a matter that most felt could have been dealt with less harshly. In February 1854, he was threatened with a knife during one of Bedern's many fights. Not for nothing did the newspapers run the regular headline – 'Another fracas in Bedern.'

Cowton was called at 1 am to break up an argument that had turned violent. He found the whole neighbourhood in the alley, but alone he entered the affray and tried to disperse it. Tempers flared and one man threatened Cowton's life. Luckily, another policeman arrived and the two of them chased who they believed were the ringleaders. Simeon Sullivan, Michael Langan and John Cade were arrested, the latter being found in a cupboard, in what the *Yorkshire Gazette* described as a 'miserable apartment, which he dignified with the title of bedroom.' The three of them were set free with a caution and Cowton swore his intention to discover the true ringleaders. Later that year, he would encounter Michael Langan once more, but not before another beating by James Tyne in October.

Cowton became a marked man and his eagerness to carry out what he saw as his duty, would simply antagonise the community.

It was 1 November and Constable Cowton was escorting a man to the police station. He was soon halted in his tracks by a large mob and from this gathering stepped Michael Langan. He attacked Cowton, wrenching his stick away from him and beating him with it. The policeman suffered terrible injuries to his face and arms, while Langan fled the town. He reappeared in the February of 1855 and was promptly arrested, fined £5 and placed in the House of Correction for two months.

Matthew Cowton was a man at breaking point. At every turn he encountered violence. On 18 August 1855, Martin McCarthy nearly choked him to death whilst resisting arrest and this catalogue of hostility continued until 1857, when matters reached a head.

The date was 27 October and at 5.30 pm that day, a coachbuilder of Goodramgate, Mr Westland, observed a man in the Bedern brandishing a knife and calling for some other men to 'come on.' Mr Westland immediately ran off in search of Constable Cowton.

The man with the knife was Thomas Lyons, a man well known to the police as a drunk and a troublemaker. Cowton arrived on the scene, but unable to deal with Lyons on his own, fetched Constable William Holmes to assist him. The two men

The old street names remain, but the Bedern slums have long gone. The Author

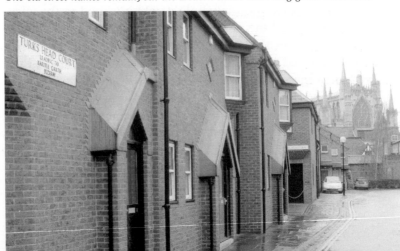

made for Lyons' home, where they found him with his equally troublesome wife, Mary. They charged him with being drunk and ordered him to accompany them to the station. Lyons had no such intention. He made a grab for a poker, but missed. Mary Lyons leapt in, lashing out at Holmes and Cowton. This gave her husband time to seize a knife and strike out, cutting Holmes across the knuckles with it. His next choice of weapon was a pan, which he rained down upon the policeman's heads. They were forced to retreat when Mary Lyons took up a pot of boiling water, launching it at them.

There was nothing left but to muster reinforcements. Within a short space of time, ten officers, including Cowton and Holmes, assembled outside the Lyons' house. Cowton had with him a crowbar, but he struggled to break open the door. Father O'Greary appeared, keen to bring about a peaceable solution. However, when he attempted to speak to Lyons through a window, the drunken Irishman shouted – 'Blood an' ounds to Father O'Greary,' and tried to strike at him. It was time to act – Cowton broke down the door and the officers rushed in.

Michael Lyons stood ready to fight, armed with a rolling pin and a pan, Mary at his side, knife in hand. The sheer force of ten burly policemen proved too much. Husband and wife bore appalling injuries, both at their home and later at the station. Police Constable Robert Duke, who dragged Mary through the streets, hit her so hard about the head with his stick that it broke in two, and this he used to beat her with again. Mary in turn, pleaded with the officers not to murder her husband.

Michael and Mary Lyons brought a case of assault and wilful damage against the officers. The magistrates believed their version of events against that of the police. They agreed that the officers had overstepped the mark, the Lyons being more assaulted than assaulting. Eight of the Constables were discharged, their guilt in the matter unclear. William Holmes was fined £2, as would Parish Constable Matthew Cowton, had he not committed suicide. Unable to face another day in the tough alleys and courtyards of the Bedern, he had taken his own life, leaving his family to seek the charity of Poor Relief once more.

Robert Chalk held on to his position until 1861, when a new Chief Constable was found in Mr Stephen Haley. By now, the police force was a much more professionally organised body, resembling the service of today. The *County and Borough Act* of 1856 had begun to standardise methods of training and procedure, enabling the forces of different towns to interact more easily. In 1874, York finally achieved parity with neighbouring forces on the issue of wages.

In 1862, Chief Constable Haley released his first statistics. The cost to the city of employing 40 constables was £2,597, the bulk of which was taken up by salaries. There had been 922 arrests in the city and 642 convictions, 61 of those for assaulting an officer. The arrests were classified under seven groups:

Male and Female known thieves	51
Vagrants	35
Suspicious characters	81
Habitual drunkards	71
Previous good character	381
Prostitutes	118

'We may gather,' wrote the *Yorkshire Gazette*, in publishing the results, 'that there still exists in our city an immense amount of vice and immorality.'

York took no pride in the fact that such a small town with a population of 40,000 boasted 64 known brothels, as well as innumerable unknown dens of sin, amongst them, 9 public houses, 8 beer shops, 6 coffee shops and 26 tramp's lodgings. Nothing, save perhaps vagrancy, offended Victorian sensibilities more. It was particularly brave of the town to acknowledge the problem. Though well aware of it, Victorians, in general, preferred to ignore prostitution in the hope that it would go away. *The Gazette* continued...

> ...*it is amongst the class to which we least allude that vice is met with in the most horrible forms. The pictures of misery and degradation to be witnessed in the hovels inhabited by the 'trulls' of Water Lane are truly appalling, while no less disgusting is the mock splendour and false adornment characterising the Cyprians of Fishergate, St John's Terrace and the surrounding quarter.*

The Magistrates or Police Courts on Clifford Street. The Author

We end with the words, printed by the *Yorkshire Gazette* and used to introduce its own publication of the police statistics for 1862. A period had passed since the formation of York's police in 1835 that saw the establishment of the railways, the introduction of the Penny Post and the telegraph, the advancement of education and parliamentary reform. The words of the Gazette reflect the feeling of having come out of the dark and entered a new age of enlightenment:

> *In all civilised communities there must be of necessity exist a*

Members of the York Constabulary, 1870. York City Libraries.

small portion of the society who are in great measure independent of public opinion. Guided by a thousand erring influences, they usually commence by becoming their own masters, and end by being the slaves to their own passions and eventually martyrs to disease. These passions seem to be undelighted amidst the delight, and joyless amidst all enjoyment; finally receiving the full measure of the punishment of their folly.

Experience speaks to such in vain, and they sink deeper into the abyss, regardless of the fearful consequences, and presenting a shocking example of the depravity of human nature. But this dark picture of mans frailty is relieved by the knowledge that 'virtue will catch as many as vice by contact; and the public stock of honest manly principle will daily accumulate.'

It is certain that a society composed of none but the wicked could not exist; it contains within itself the seeds of its own destruction, and would be swept away from the face of the earth by the deluge of its own iniquity. The rottenness in the state would soon be past remedy, and the poor decayed remnants of a great nation would pass away and 'leave no sign.'

The life of a malefactor fills the storybooks with heroes, and soon the person himself is held up to the fear and abhorrence of the juvenile inmates of the nursery. The crimes are retailed with extravagant additions, and have also been the source of subjects for the author and the artist. A glance at the relics of noted criminals to be seen in York Castle awakens in the mind of the octogenarian, recollections of a state of society far different to what it is now. But luckily that period is past, and though we do not rejoice in a state of fabulous honesty said to have existed in the reign of Alfred, yet we have reason for self-congratulation at the efficiency of our police, and the completeness of their functions. It has been, and ever will be, lawful to attack vice, and a well regulated body of police seem to be perfectly adapted to the present condition of society and its vicious tendencies. Our own good city is not exempt from evils, and a large constabulary find plenty of work.

In 1968, the York Police Force joined with the North Riding Constabulary. Cyril Carter was the city's final Chief Constable and his name survives on this notice near Lendal Bridge. The Author

Chapter 9

Poor Horatio

Hungate: 1884

Bordered on two sides by the River Foss, Hungate has hardly had the most salubrious of histories. Its old Viking name of *Dunnyndykes* comes from it being used as a dumping site for animal dung and between the twelfth and fifteenth centuries it was little more than a public tip, particularly for the butchers and slaughter men of the Shambles. This gave rise to the name, *Hundegat in Mersch*, or The Dog's Street in the Marsh, from all the prowling strays that inhabited the area. Perhaps Hungate contributed to the unbearable stench that King Edward the Third endured when he visited the city – and he was used to the smell of the fourteenth century. From these filthy beginnings, one might imagine that Hungate could only improve. Most would argue that it did not.

The flood waters recede in Lower Wesley Place by the Foss in Hungate. York City Archives.

As we walk through York's streets today, it is hard to imagine what life inside the city walls meant to a great deal of its citizens in the nineteenth century. As the population increased from 17,000 in 1800, to 40,000 in 1850, they sought housing within walking distance of employment and the largest source of that was domestic service. The industrial boom that built up the likes of Sheffield, Leeds and Bradford for the most part missed York. The Rowntree's factory, which by 1914 would employ more than 4,000, had a workforce of 100 in 1879. Even the railways, could not compete in terms of the number of domestic employees, having little more than 1,200 men at the works in 1855.

Between 1821 and 1841 the number of houses in the city increased by sixty per cent, mostly of a poor type. They built back-to-back courtyard developments, crammed together, where a dozen families would be forced to share a single standpipe and one midden privy. In general, the houses had two rooms – one up, one down – while many single storey, single room cottages housed whole families in dark, damp conditions. Several homes had a pigsty or stable attached to them and slaughter yards shared courtyards with private houses.

The midden privy was an archaic contrivance, little more than a wooden seat fixed above a dry pit. Once the night soil had accumulated it was barrowed into the street and from there

Foss Bridge, between Fossgate and Walmgate. The Author

taken to huge dung heaps in the town, ready for sale to the farmers. In Fossgate, on the border of Hungate, a particularly huge mound famously stood by Foss Bridge filling the air with its reek. Although this particular practice was halted, the city had 5,000 such privies still in use at the turn of the twentieth century.

Navigation and damming work on the River Foss had forced its levels up by two metres above that of the Ouse and its flow had virtually ceased. Most sewers were little more than open gutters; in fact no closed drainage of any worth had been laid since the time of the Romans. The waste of Hungate and Fossgate emptied into the stagnated river, which in times of flood spilled its putrid contents back into the streets and houses. No surprise then that the city failed to avoid the cholera epidemic that was sweeping the country in 1831. The Central Board of Health reported in that year...

...by this great defect, houses, dung heaps, pig sties etc which unfortunately subsist in the heart of town, and represented as pouring their fetid contents into open drains and the effluvia to be sometime such as might alone suffice to generate contagion.

It began in Beedhams Court (known as Hagworm's Nest), off Skeldersgate, when impoverished ferryman, Thomas Hughes, fell ill on 2 June 1832. Though he lived, the disease spread to his family and neighbours, and then quickly across the river into the filth of the Water Lanes. From there, it came upon the Shambles, Swann Street and Hungate. In 1832, of the 500 reported cases across the city, 185 lost their lives, many being buried outside the walls, in Thief Lane. In the words of the *York Herald*:

The pestilence (like a thief in the night) silently and unobserved entered the city, and took up its deadly stand on the vitals of the vitiated and in the dwellings of the more virtuous poor...

The cholera hit again in 1847 alongside an outbreak of typhus in Walmgate and as late as 1886, typhoid raged through the poorer districts. The death rate in York was well above the national average throughout the nineteenth century. In 1888, infant mortality was recorded as being 287 deaths for every 1,000 births.

The gravestone of William Trotter in York Cemetery tells a sorry tale, but sadly not out of the ordinary. The Author

The city's dreadful mortality rate paid little attention to status. Prior to his death in 1896, former Lord Mayor, John Close, had buried two wives and eight children – six of those before their first birthdays. The Author

Improvements in sanitation were slow to appear; after all the money owning classes had begun to gravitate outwards towards The Mount, Heworth, Fulford and Clifton. The gentry, by the middle of the century, had left the city, unwilling to live side by side with their poorer neighbours as their Georgian fathers had done. Abandoned houses and mansions were stripped out and turned into warehouses and tenements.

The *Public Health Act* of 1872 was implemented slowly, frequently tied up by the committee system favoured by the Victorians, and York's slums festered on until after the Great War and beyond.

Something of Hungate's decline can be seen in the trade directories. In 1823, there appeared a wealth of makers of wheels, mattresses, cabinets, hats, saddles and thread. Tailors worked alongside Bakers, Cutlers and Wine Merchants. In *White's Directory* of 1840, skilled professions have decreased dramatically, leaving a Cattle Dealer, Baker, Fishmonger, Coal

Merchant and ever-present Brewer. At the end of the century, shopkeepers prevail, while Leetham's Flour Mill at the connection of the Foss and Wormould's Cut and the gas works provide the main employment.

In the Medical Health Officer's report on sanitary conditions in York for 1884, he describes Hungate as a

> *...poor district, lying low. The inhabitants are for the most part poor persons, labourers and others of the humbler classes of working men. There are many associated privies and water closets in the district. Some are back to back houses; many courts and yards. There are no tenement houses and no common lodging houses. The locality is damp, and the general ventilation is not good. There is less cleanliness and less comfort than in any of the other districts, and more evidence of poverty.*

In his letter to the Local Government Board in London, he names Hungate as the 'worst part of the city.' Not an easy place to live.

In January 1884, a twenty-six-year-old mother by the name of Elizabeth Palmer is living in a single room in Hungate with her two-year-old son, Horatio Lambert. The boy had been born in the Leeds Workhouse and up until recently, Elizabeth had been employed at the home of Mr Charles Simpson in nearby

Designed by John Carr in 1780, Castlegate House is typical of the housing abandoned during the early nineteenth century. The Author

Leetham's Flour Mill provided employment to many of Hungate's residents. The Author

Pavement. However, due to what he described as her 'curious ideas' he was forced to let her go.

Life for a single mother in the slums was never going to be easy and Elizabeth struggled. Horatio was cutting his teeth, he had a cold, and with the added pain of hunger, he spent much of his time crying. The child was often left with Sarah Gamble, a builder's wife, while she visited the alehouses, not returning home until she was drunk. Many such 'alehouses' were little more than grimy ground floor rooms capable of holding no more than a dozen people, where the landlord would open his doors before 9 am, and shut them when the money ran out.

At the start of February, Horatio became quiet. More than that, he had not been seen for several days. Elizabeth was acting more strangely than usual and her neighbours grew concerned for the boy's safety. Then, following a passing statement she made to a shopkeeper, the police were called in. Police Constable Thornton visited Elizabeth to make enquiries and was shocked by what he heard. When he asked about Horatio's whereabouts, he was told,

'In the River Ouse. I didn't throw it in.'

When he asked who did, Elizabeth replied,

'A woman in Walmgate named Lambert.'

Back at the police station, Chief Constable Haley interviewed Elizabeth, but she was so distressed that he thought she was unlikely to make much sense. When Doctor Marshall examined her he diagnosed insanity. Taken before the magistrates at the Guildhall, she was charged with 'maliciously murdering her child named Horatio Lambert.' The case was postponed to allow the police time to make more enquiries and when asked if she had anything to say, Elizabeth replied,

'The child is drowned.'

As she left the courtroom, she called out, seemingly to someone in the gallery.

'Cheer up, the Lord is with me yet.'

For nearly a week, Detective Sergeant Denham headed the search for Horatio but further investigations made in Hungate revealed no clues. The Ouse was dragged but the height of the river made it impossible to proceed. Subsequently, on 13 February, Elizabeth stood in the Guildhall once more to hear the charge of 'wilful murder' made against her.

Despite the fact that she had admitted that Horatio had been thrown into the river, there was no body. What's more, a doctor had expressed the opinion that she was insane. The Lord Mayor and

Pavement, looking towards St Saviours Church. The Author

Garden Place, Hungate. The tower of St Saviours Church can just be seen above the roofs. York City Archives

St Saviours Church in Hungate, now home to the Archaeological Resource Centre. The Author

Alderman Terry inquired if Elizabeth had any friends in York. Perhaps they intended to send her to them, but Detective Sergeant Denham did not think that she had any. The Clerk of the Court, Mr Munby, then asked Elizabeth if she knew of any reason why she should not be remanded. At first it seemed that she would not answer, but after a brief silence she spoke.

'I recollect something about it. I have been two years in bed since that. I have been asleep. It seems like a dream.'

She was asked no more questions and did not speak again. Remanded in custody, Elizabeth was returned to the workhouse, and from there, under a certificate of lunacy, to the asylum.

Three weeks passed without change and then by chance the naked body of a child was found in the River Ouse at Barlby, near Selby. Two days later in *The Hare and Hounds* at Ricall, Mr Taylor, the Wakefield Coroner, held an inquest.

Dr Vincent Wanostrocht, who had examined the body, told the jury that in his opinion it had never been clothed during the time it had been in the water. The child's identity was next called to question.

Elizabeth's sister, Mary Ann Palmer, of Green Lane, Brayton, viewed the corpse and confirmed that it was Horatio, as did Sarah Gamble, but the jury were not convinced. They returned an open verdict of 'Found Drowned,' and although they considered it most probable that the child was Horatio, the evidence was inconclusive. The body had been in the water for three weeks and it is doubtful whether anyone could swear without a trace of doubt that it was Horatio. Without this, Elizabeth Palmer could not stand trial, and being insane, neither would she hang if she did. For her, there was only the obscurity of life in the asylum with her tortured thoughts to keep her awake at night.

Whether the woman named Lambert ever existed (Horatio's surname was also Lambert) no mention was ever made. Perhaps she was the person in the Guildhall gallery whom Elizabeth had called to. Possibly she had been coerced into committing murder, having been convinced that she would never find employment, of any type, with a child in tow. Walmgate was a well-known haunt of prostitutes, and for a woman in Elizabeth's predicament it may have seemed a way out. Then again, perhaps she was simply insane, driven further into that insanity by the hardships of slum life.

It took a Quaker family to spell out the problems that many of those governing York's public services already knew; that the city was in a sordid state. Seebohm Rowntree's study of 1899 showed that more than fifteen per cent of the working class population lived in poverty. Sixty per cent of their homes were only 'tolerable', while the slums counted for twenty six per cent of all working class housing. The Rowntree family at least began to

work towards improving conditions with the building of New Earswick in 1902. Based on a rural style (perhaps even idyll), the houses in the garden village must have seemed like palaces to their new occupants. It would be a design not just copied by York City Council for its own housing project at Tang Hall, but by others throughout the country at places like Letchworth and Welwyn Garden City. The city that boasted slums as shocking as anywhere in the whole of the country went some way to providing an answer, even if it was slow to practice the methods.

The acceptable face of Hungate – St Saviourgate. The Author

Chapter 10

Murder on Hope Street
Walmgate: 1883

So many of the Irish immigrants who arrived in York in the middle of the nineteenth century found the welcome they received, tepid, if not cold and hostile. Prejudice among the city's long-standing residents ran deep and it did not help that community feuds, instead of being left behind in the old country, came with them. The difficulties that this caused provided the authorities with countless problems and led on occasion to near riot. They came as refugees to help build, work on the railways and to labour in the fields, but to many, including much of the local press, they came to beg, to thieve and to idle away their days fighting and drinking. They were little better than gypsies, attracted to York's thriving fairs and markets or any gathering that lent itself to pocket picking and hawking, and what's more – they were foreigners.

Nearly half of all the immigrants settled in the Walmgate district, in hastily developed courtyards behind abundant inns and public houses, or in tightly packed terraces of depressingly small houses. One such street, Hope Street, had a large concentration of Irish and in 1873, a young man named Martin Kivell, married a girl by the name of Mary Conney. Martin was Irish by descent, but Mary was a York girl who had grown up in Hope Street and though not unheard of, it was a situation that some would have found intolerable. The couple made their home in 23 Hope Street, a house with a kitchen and front room on the ground floor and two bedrooms upstairs. Martin was a good worker and he diligently plied his trade as a bricklayer's labourer. In the year of their marriage, the couples first child was born, a girl whom they named Mary Ann and on 18 October 1875, a baby boy, James, the apple of his father's eye.

1880 found Martin employed on building work being carried out at Victoria Bar Chapel near Nunnery Lane, and it was here that tragedy struck. He fell from the scaffolding, receiving severe

Old Hope Street. Looking towards Walmgate, the Brown Cow *public house is on the right.* York City Archives.

Victoria Bar Chapel. The Author

head injuries and for a time his situation was so critical that it was feared he might not live. Recovery was slow and though his physical condition improved, it was his mental state that gave cause for concern. It took him about six months to fully regain his health, with some of that time being spent in the asylum. On his return to the family home, life as a labourer in York had lost its appeal and a new life beckoned. He would have heard the stories of his fellow countrymen and their great riches in America. The grass being greener over the water, he believed that New York offered him the chance to improve his lot. So without too much delay, he packed his bag and left.

During the two years that Martin worked in America, he wrote regularly to Mary, and when he could, he included money. Not enough, however, to support his young family and so Mary was forced to take in lodgers. She moved into the front bedroom with the children and soon after Martin's departure, rented out the back room to an Irish labourer, John Gallagher. Other lodgers came and went, sharing the room with John, but he remained for two years. Then, in 1883, Martin grew tired of America, having found that the grass was as jaded as old York, and he returned home.

On his arrival, he removed one of the lodgers from the house, but he seemed happy to let John Gallagher keep his room. This arrangement continued for a week and there were no arguments in that time, not between Martin and John, nor husband and wife. Until the night of Monday, 10 December all appeared as well as it might have been.

On that night, Mary put James to bed shortly after 9 pm. As she tucked him beneath his blanket, the boy said, 'I shan't go to sleep until you come to bed. Don't sleep in my Dada's bed, I am very frightened of my Dada.'

James had been five years old when his father had left. His memory of him would be vague and very possibly he was having trouble accepting this virtual stranger who had entered the house. Mary did not reply to her son. Martin had given her no reason to be fearful of him and things were bound to be strained at first. She joined her husband and John by the fireside in the back kitchen, but Martin left them, going out to the woodshed in the back yard. Having chopped an armful of wood, he stacked the fire to the top of the grate. Not happy with the result, he took two shovels of coal and threw them on top of the wood, creating a blaze fit to burn the house down. Sometime between 11pm and midnight he asked Mary if she was going to bed.

'Martin, wait a minute,' replied Mary, wanting to wait until the fire had died down, but this reply caused Martin to suddenly snap.

'Either go up to bed, or get out,' he said.

She did neither, so Martin grabbed her hands, dragged her across the kitchen and threw her out, locking the door behind her. Mary ran out into the street, hoping to locate a policeman. Two neighbours returning home, John Connery and Tom Habit agreed to guard the house, while she searched. Outside the *Spotted Dog* public house, she came across three officers, one of whom happened to be Inspector Masterman and Mary told him how frightened she was. How her husband, who was once in an asylum, had built a huge fire in the grate and locked her out of the house – and her with two children in their bed's. Inspector Masterman, used to dealing with the domestic squabbles of Walmgate, quickly ascertained that her children were not alone

The Brown Cow, *Hope Street. Same name, new building.* The Author

in the house, there being a lodger. Mary, not so easily placated, asked that they come and protect the house, telling them that if they did, she would have her husband examined to see if he was still insane. Masterman calmly informed her that she would have to apply to the Relieving Officer for that purpose. Mary returned promptly to Hope Street, believing that the policemen would follow, but as far as Inspector Masterman was concerned the matter had been dealt with.

The two men that Mary had left guarding the house were still there when she returned and they waited with her for half an hour, but the expected policemen never showed. Though Mary was desperate to get her children out, she eventually gave up and made her way to the home of her aunt, Bridgett Panett, also in Hope Street. Mary's mother lived in the same road, but she thought that this was the first place Martin would come looking for a fight. She did not return home until Tuesday morning.

John Gallagher's recollection of that Monday evening differs slightly from Mary Kivell's. According to him, Mary was turned out of the house between 8-9 pm. He confirmed that Martin had built a fearsome fire, but that when he (Gallagher) retired at 9.15 pm, young James was not in bed. The boy was in the kitchen with his father and shortly afterwards came upstairs to his room. John heard Martin tell James to be a good boy and bid him goodnight. Whichever of them is true, the events that followed are in no dispute.

At some point later that evening, Martin got his daughter, Mary Ann, out of bed and sent her out to find her mother. On his instructions she went to another of her mother's aunts, Mrs Conney, but returned without success. Convinced that she was there, Martin then went himself and finding that she was not, went home without checking at other members of Mary's family. After midnight he sent Mary Ann out into the streets again, but once more she failed to find her mother. For a third time she went to search, being told this time not to come home without her. Like her mother, the girl did not come home again until Tuesday morning.

John Gallagher claimed that he did not sleep well, so worried was he about Mary and Mary Ann. At 7.15 am on Tuesday morning he heard Martin Kivell go down stairs and walk about the kitchen in his boots for a quarter hour. He then came back to the front bedroom and woke James up. John heard Martin telling his son that he would have to be a good boy and go to school. He heard nothing else; no shouts, no bangs, no arguments, no fighting, nothing until he heard James shout – 'Oh Father!'

John descended the stairs in a rush and in the kitchen he saw Martin stood above the slumped form of his son. James Kivell was laid on the stone floor in a pool of fresh blood. His head was resting on a block of wood and a deep gash had nearly severed it from his body. Behind the mute figure of Martin lay a blood-smeared axe; the very one he had used to chop wood with on the previous night. John asked him twice what he had done, but Martin did not speak, or move. In silence he stared at the figure of his lifeless son.

John Gallagher dressed quickly and ran to the police station. Inspector William Steel, accompanied by a constable came straight away, arriving at 23 Hope Street at 7.45 pm. There they found the grisly sight of the boy lying across the chopping block, wearing only his nightshirt. The murderer was nowhere to be seen. Having made a quick search of the house, they ran into the road and promptly apprehended Martin at the junction of Hope and George Street, not one hundred and eighty metres from the house.

Under arrest at the police station, Martin made only one statement – 'I don't know what made me do it.'

Mary Kivell learnt from a neighbour that the police were guarding her door, and from them the fate of her child.

The coroner's inquest was held the very next day at St Peter's Vaults in Walmgate. Mr J Marshall, a surgeon from St Saviourgate described James Kivell's injuries:

> *I found a wound four inches in extent, dividing the tissues of the bone on the forehead and top of the head, also a bruise on the right cheek and ear. On the left side of the neck, at the base of the skull, there was a wound five inches in extent and separating the spinal cord from the skull; also a more superficial wound about two inches in extent near to the deeper wound. Either of the two wounds first described is sufficient to have caused death.*

Not a single blow then, nor a moment of anger taken to extremes. Martin had felled his son with a blow, possibly two, to

Old Hope Street looking towards George Street. York City Archives

the head and then laid that head against the chopping block and finished the terrible act with a full swipe of the axe.

Recent changes to the law meant that Martin was not allowed to attend the inquest without a special order, and so Detective Frank Denham visited Martin in the castle gaol. Denham asked him if he wanted to make a statement at the inquest in front of the jury. Martin's reply was, 'No, Frank, I don't wish to make a statement.'

It was now time for the coroner to sum up:

There is no evidence I think of before us of premeditation on the part of the man, but all homicide is presumed to be malicious unless there is evidence of circumstances of alleviation, excuse, or justification. Now there is no evidence, I think you will be of the opinion, before you of any such excuse as that, and it is for you to say, on the evidence you have heard, whether you consider that the father of this lad did wilfully and maliciously cause his death... I may tell you that you have nothing to do with the state of Kivell's mind.

It took the jury twenty five minutes to return a verdict of 'Wilful Murder,' against Martin Kivell, and he would now await the spring assizes. Insanity would keep the rope from his neck.

Between the years of 1929 and 1931, Hope Street as it was then, was demolished.

Modern-day Hope Street. The Author

Chapter 11

The Killing of John Dalby

Alma Terrace: 1904

Edmund Hall was the kind of man who felt that life owed him more than it gave him. Not that he was lazy; his employers, Greenwood and Batley at the Allen ammunition factory in Leeds, spoke highly of him. An attentive worker, they said, who had never missed a minute of work in all the time he had been with them. Of course, the death of his wife, Hannah, in July 1903, had been a tragedy: herself a widow when she married Edmund and only in her 40's when she died. A tragedy indeed and perhaps it was this event that sparked his money troubles, causing him to turn to his deceased wife's family and beg for their help.

In February 1904, he turned up on the doorstep of 14 Newgate, York; a shoe shop belonging to Francis Plummer Chatwin. Mr Chatwin was married to the sister of Edmund's

Now a jewellers, 14 Newgate, the Dalby family shoe shop. The Author

late wife and together they ran the little shop. Husband and wife worked long hours, keen to make a success of the business built up by Mrs Chatwin's father, John Dalby. Edmund told them that he was desperate. The bailiffs were in his house at Leeds and he needed money, either given or borrowed, it did not matter which. Could Mrs Chatwin find pity in her heart for her brother-in-law? Edmund certainly thought so – but he was wrong. Francis Chatwin refused to loan him a penny and asked him to leave the property forthwith. Perhaps it was his brusque nature, or that he was no longer considered a close enough family member to receive its charity; but Edmund left York intent on returning.

On 29 July, Frederick Parkinson was going about his usual business as sales assistant with Lindley Brothers, gunmakers of Leeds. A man entered who wished to purchase a revolver. He told Parkinson that his son was going to Canada for six months and needed a firearm for the trip. Unfortunately, as he had no license, Parkinson could not sell him one. He did though, provide him with a letter, which read:

> *Mr James Smith is going to Canada for a period of not less than six months and wishes to purchase a revolver.*

If Mr Smith was to present this note at a police station, he could obtain a license and then buy his gun. Mr Smith left the shop, but did not make his way to a police station; neither did he have a son bound for Canada, because Edmund Hall had no son. Edmund Hall simply wished to arm himself with a bargaining tool for when he next met with his wife's family. No matter, the finely honed knife in his overcoat pocket would do just as well. From the gun shop, he made straight for the railway station and caught the York train.

John Dalby was seventy-eight years old, a retired boot maker and shoe seller. He lived at 4 Alma Terrace, about one and a half kilometres from the city centre, just off the Fulford Road. It was a good address; built in the late nineteenth century it ran down towards the River Ouse and provided housing for that rank of person who had risen above the ordinary working class. Shopkeepers, managers and owners of small family concerns, just like the one built up by John Dalby, now capably operated

Alma Terrace. The Author

The New Walk along the Ouse as it passes Alma Terrace. The Author

by his son-in-law and daughter.

He lived a good life and was an easy going, affable chap; still fit enough to take his strolls along the river on the New Walk, meeting his friends, watching the boats and on occasion heading into town to visit the shop.

It was just before 9 pm on 29 July and Mrs Broadley had returned the laundry. She stayed about five minutes, chatted, and then left John to carry on preparing the evening meal. The Chatwins would be returning soon from a long day and tonight he was cooking a fine joint of beef. But his daily routine was about to be interrupted.

Outside 4 Alma Terrace, thirteen year old Gertrude Liddle stood kicking her heels, waiting for a friend to arrive. A man approached and knocked at the door. Noticing that he got no reply, she called – 'He's a bit deaf, you'll have to knock louder.' The stranger did so and sure enough the door opened.

'Edmund,' greeted John Dalby warmly. 'Have you been to the shop?'

'Not yet,' replied Edmund Hall stepping across the doorstep. As he did so, Francis Chatwin was locking the Newgate premises. His wife chose to catch the tramcar, while he decided to walk home along the riverbank to Alma Terrace.

At 9.15 pm, Martha Jagger of 3 Alma Terrace, heard noises coming from number 4. It sounded like a scuffle, then the breaking of crockery and finally a voice, she knew to be John Dalby's, groaning. She ran from the house and knocked at the door of John Liddle's at number 2, at the same moment, her husband, also called John, came down the street, returning from work.

'Oh, Jack,' she cried. 'Do go to Dalby's; there's something awful going on.'

John Liddle and John Jagger banged at the door of number 4. Hearing noises within, they tried to force the lock without success. From the rear of number 3, they scaled the wall into Dalby's yard and tried the back door, but that too was locked. As both men attempted to open a window, the back door suddenly opened and there propped against it was John Dalby, streaming in blood. Liddle hurried forward and supported him. The old man tried to speak, but he was choked with the blood of his opened throat. Liddle called out for someone to fetch a

The door to Number 4. The Author

doctor and the police. John Jagger grabbed a nearby chair and lowered Dalby into it, who was still trying desperately to make his message understood. Then, from the middle room of the house, a man suddenly appeared. He forced his way through, shouting – 'I'll fetch a doctor,' and promptly climbed the yard wall and was gone.

'Stop that man, Liddle,' said Jagger and Liddle set off in pursuit. Unable to track him, he fetched Police Sergeant Charles Selby from the Alma Terrace station.

Meanwhile Jagger had laid John Dalby down and supported his head with a cushion. This seemed to clear his throat and he

The former Alma Terrace Police Station. The Author

was able to speak.

'My son-in-law from Leeds has robbed me and taken my watch and chain.' He pushed his fingers into his empty waistcoat pocket. 'I was getting his supper ready.'

Sergeant Selby's arrival was closely followed by that of Dr William Flood. He attempted to ease the blood loss, inserting forty stitches through the wound on poor Dalby's throat. Into this terrible scene walked his daughter and her husband. The time was 9.30 pm.

Headed by Detective Inspector Morrell, a manhunt was set in motion. Francis Chatwin joined the search, being able to

Inspector Morrell. Author's collectio

identify Edmund Hall. They found him at 11 pm. He was sat on a train, due to leave for Leeds at 11.10 pm. A blue muffler scarf wrapped around his neck, he had attempted a disguise by wearing spectacles, but there was no mistaking his sallow complexion and jet-black bushy moustache. In his mouth,

Designed by Thomas Prosser, York Railway Station has changed little since it opened in 1877. The Author

smouldered a huge cigar; Edmund Hall obviously thought his escape was guaranteed.

At the Clifford Street police station, a search of his clothing revealed the stolen watch, eleven shillings and sixpence in cash and the letter introducing him to the Leeds police as James Smith. The sleeves of his coat were wet, where he had scrubbed the bloody evidence from them. However, bloodstains remained on his shirt and handkerchief. The murder weapon was nowhere to be found; no doubt it was at the bottom of the river.

The following day, John Jagger picked Edmund from a line up of fifteen men as the man he had seen exit Alma Terrace ostensibly in search of a doctor.

'I have done nothing,' insisted Edmund, 'and I want to know why I have been brought here.'

On Saturday, 30 July at 11 pm, John Dalby lost his fight for life in the city hospital and the charge of 'attempted murder' became one of 'willful murder'.

The coroner's inquest, the magistrates nor the jury at the assizes in December believed Edmund Hall to be as innocent as he claimed. Found guilty of murder, he was sentenced to hang. The famous and often, though not on this occasion, eccentric Justice Darling called it, 'a murder committed under circumstances of great barbarity.' The prisoner held his silence throughout.

At 6 am on Tuesday, 20 December 1904, Edmund rose from his bed in Armley Gaol and ate a substantial breakfast. During his incarceration he had remained a taciturn man, seemingly resigned to his fate. Wesleyan Minister, Reverend Paul Ellis, described him as 'a bright spirit,' a man fully prepared 'to meet his doom.'

At 9 am, a procession left the condemned cell. Two warders, two priests, Alderman Bentley, the Sheriff of York and the Under-Sheriff, Mr Rymer, accompanied the hangman, John Billington and his assistant, Henry Pierepoint, to the scaffold.

Edmund Hall's final wish was that a young cousin of his continue to be a good lad – 'Not only as a soldier of the King, but of Jesus Christ, as I have been.'

Chapter 12

The Mystery at 5¹/₂

The Crescent: 1904

J ust before Blossom Street squeezes through the confines of Micklegate, a quiet unassuming sweep of Victorian terrace houses, The Crescent, offers solitude away from the bustle of what was York's busiest approach. An opening halfway down the terrace, between numbers 5 and 6, leads to a workshop. Today a joiner's yard, but in 1904, Mr George Shearsmith operated his gunsmith's business from the premises.

On the morning of Friday, 30 December 1904, a young apprentice of Shearsmith's by the name of Fred Stone stood looking at a board of keys on the workshop wall. One of the keys belonged to the

George Shearsmith
Author's collection

The Crescent as it appeared at the turn of the century. The entrance to Shearsmith's Yard is halfway down on the left. Author's collection

5¹/₂ The Crescent. The Author

Blacksmith's shop and Mrs Isabella Hewitt used it when she went in to tidy the place up. Worried that Mrs Hewitt had not been seen for a couple of days, Fred arranged the key in a particular way, so that he would know if it had been moved – and it had not.

The Hewitt's, William and Isabella, had lived in York for ten years, having come from Hull. William had been an engineers turner with the North Eastern Railway Company until his recent retirement at the age of seventy-three. For the last seven years, the couple had rented number 5¹/₂ The Crescent. The address was a humble two-roomed cottage in the gunsmith's yard, overlooked by the three storey houses of the street outside. They were an everyday couple, well liked by former colleagues, neighbours and a young apprentice wondering why Isabella's key had not been used.

Crossing the yard to the cottage, Fred Stone knocked at the door without success. The curtains were drawn but he could just see inside, and what he saw made him run for the police. William Hewitt was face down on the floor, while his wife lay on the couch, a bloody cloth covering her battered face. As Fred told the police, there was blood everywhere and 'brains scattered about.'

Fred Stone.
Author's collection

Sergeant Bain attended and he gained entry through a partly open window, the door being locked from the inside. The scene that awaited them was as ghastly as Fred had described.

William had been severely hit about the head and his face was smeared in cinder ash and mud. Isabella had suffered the most horrendous beating. The right side of her face was crushed beyond recognition, her throat slit, and all about, the walls smattered with blood.

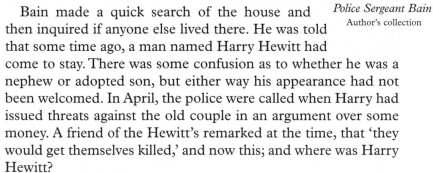

Police Sergeant Bain
Author's collection

Bain made a quick search of the house and then inquired if anyone else lived there. He was told that some time ago, a man named Harry Hewitt had come to stay. There was some confusion as to whether he was a nephew or adopted son, but either way his appearance had not been welcomed. In April, the police were called when Harry had issued threats against the old couple in an argument over some money. A friend of the Hewitt's remarked at the time, that 'they would get themselves killed,' and now this; and where was Harry Hewitt?

A description of him was issued immediately and the city's constables told to be on lookout. Friday went by without any reported sightings and Saturday the same, until 8.30 pm that night. Constable Southwood was guarding the Hewitt's cottage, when a man entered the yard. Dressed in a long overcoat and wearing a brown hat, hands pushed deep in his pockets, he made straight towards Southwood.

'Who goes there?' demanded Southwood.

'Harry Hewitt,' came the reply.

'What do you want here?' said the policeman.

'Oh nothing,' replied Hewitt, casually. 'Just looking around.'

Without delay, the constable clamped him in handcuffs and marched him towards the police station. Passers-by, seeing the two men, quickly realised what was happening and very soon, a crowd gathered at the door of the station. Many had been attending the coroner's inquest in the schoolroom on Queens Street. Hewitt, however, had not come to confess his crimes, because when questioned he would neither implicate himself or deny his involvement. At no time did he ask why he was being arrested.

The entrance to Shearsmith's Yard. The Author

On Monday, 2 January 1905, Harry Hewitt stood in the packed Police Court to answer the charge of 'suspicion of wilful murder.' As the Chief Constable issued the instruction, 'Put up Hewitt,' the accused entered the dock and leaning slovenly on the bar, rested his whiskered chin in his hand. One journalist described him as having a 'Wild West' look, with his roughly combed hair and great growths of bedraggled beard. Another thought him a 'physiognomical mystery,' in other words, one whose character is difficult to judge from their outward appearance.

The hearing in which the prisoner was described as a chemist, aged forty (in fact he was thirty-five), was over in minutes and Hewitt left the dock without so much as a word.

The funeral of William and Isabella Hewitt took place the next day. Joining relatives and members of the Society of Engineers, were 7,500 people lining the street to watch the cortège enter the City Cemetery. The Society of Engineers met the costs of the funeral and ten of its pensioners bore the coffins into the chapel. Meanwhile, in York Gaol, their 'adopted son' awaited his appearance in the Magistrates Court.

The cemetery gates. The Author

York City Cemetery Chapel. The Author

Mr Lucas and Mr Wilkinson would conduct his case, though Harry, despite pleading not guilty deferred his defence. The Director of Public Prosecutions had entrusted Mr Cecil Cobb with the job of dealing with what was very circumstantial evidence.

The murder weapons had been found in the cottage. A large wooden mallet hidden in a wash basket, and a bloodstained knife wrapped in a rag. Neither of them could be shown as belonging to Harry Hewitt, and the blood on both might or might not belong to the murdered couple. Much was made of a blood stained axe found at the scene, but the police discounted it, presumably because the wounds found on the Hewitt's did not match those formed by an axe. Cecil Cobb would, therefore, have to provide a plausible motive for the killing. He called Police Constable Wand and questioned him over the disturbance in the April of 1904.

On that day, Isabella Hewitt called for the police because she was frightened of Harry: so frightened that she had taken to sleeping in a shed in the yard. William, who had attempted to stand up to Harry, was lame following the altercation. During the course of her conversation with Constable Wand, Isabella repeatedly made reference to Harry being illegitimate and in the end, the policeman asked her to be quiet about it.

'He thinks we are receiving money from his people that we ought not to have,' complained Isabella.

'I know you have,' said Harry, who had been without work for some three years. He trained out as a chemist with Shillito's on Lord Mayor's Walk, and then moved to Castleford in the same employment, eventually losing his position there. Cobb seized upon the following words spoken by Harry to Constable Wand, suggesting that they were an indication of malicious intent.

'One get's into queer streets sometimes. There never would have been any trouble but for my Father, who is in London. I know for a fact that they get money for me, and they wanted to stop the clock on me, but I wouldn't have it. They have not done as they ought or things would have been different.'

However, the Hewitt's were not receiving money from Harry's family and supporting the unemployed chemist had put them in debt. The rent on the cottage, set at 3s and 6d a week, was in

Lord Mayor's Walk. The Author

arrears to a sum in excess of £14. William received 16s a week from two pensions, which should have been enough to provide a modest living.

With a motive apparently found, Cobb needed to place Harry at the scene of the crime. William Metcalf, who worked at the *Station Hotel*, came forward, believing that he had seen the murderer.

The Crescent. The Author

Metcalf left work on Wednesday, 28 December at around midnight. Walking home to East Mount Parade, he passed The Crescent at 12.15 am and heard a man crying, 'Don't, don't.' There was a shuffling sound, followed by the shutting of a door and five minutes later, a man appeared out of the passageway. He walked quickly on the opposite path to the witness, rounded the cabstand, and made towards Micklegate. Metcalf, who had found it necessary to wait those five minutes after hearing the cry, did not follow the man; neither did he hail for a policeman, or investigate the entrance to Shearsmith's yard. When asked if he could identify Harry Hewitt as the fleeing man, Metcalf said that he could not, in fact his description of him was no more detailed than 'he wore a Billycock' (a felt hat similar to a Derby) and a long overcoat. Metcalf's statement was at odds with the findings of the police surgeon.

Dr Harry William Reynolds described to the court the wounds found on the deceased and gave his opinion of how they were received. William Hewitt was attacked outside in the yard and then dragged by the feet, face down, into the cottage. As well as the injuries to the head, his hands were damaged either by being stamped on, or while trying to defend himself. In total, he had been subjected to ten or eleven blows. Isabella Hewitt died as a result of being hit around the head and afterwards, her throat cut with a kitchen knife. Reynolds believed that she had been asleep the whole time. There were no signs of a struggle and it would have been impossible to lift Isabella, she being a large woman, onto the sofa – for one man at least. Furthermore, an empty gin bottle, found close to the body, suggested that she might have been under the influence. According to the surgeon's calculations, the attack would have lasted half an hour.

In his statement, William Metcalf had said that only five minutes passed between him hearing the cry, 'Don't, don't,' presumably made by William Hewitt, and seeing the man exit the yard. Five minutes in which to rain eleven blows on the old man, drag his body inside, deliver five more blows to Isabella, cut her throat, hide the mallet and knife, lock the door and leave through the window. Add to this, the evidence that the killer had used the kitchen sink, perhaps to wash his hands, and five minutes seems too short a time. Either Metcalf was mistaken

Linton Bridge on the River Wharfe. The Author

about the length of time that he had stood waiting, hearing the cry, or the unidentified man leaving The Crescent was not the murderer. Other witnesses had no trouble identifying Harry Hewitt.

At 12.30 pm on the Wednesday, twenty-eight year old, Walter Christie was on Linton Bridge, just outside Wetherby, when, or so he thought, Harry Hewitt approached him and asked if he could help an out of work man. Christie gave him tuppence and Hewitt walked away in the direction of Wetherby. Later that same day, John Hobson swore that the accused entered the *Sun Inn* at Long Marston and that he had bought him a pint of beer, receiving an ornamental walking stick in thanks. The North Eastern Railway Company had presented the stick to William Hewitt at Christmas 1903.

Harry Hewitt made no response to these two statements; not until further witnesses started to place him closer to number 5$\frac{1}{2}$ did he speak.

George Davies, a shopkeeper on Poppleton Road, claimed that Hewitt called at his premises on Wednesday evening, asking for a drink of water.

The Sun Inn *at Long Marston, between Wetherby and York.* The Author

'I think he has made a mistake,' said Harry to the courtroom.

Then, Francis Lawson swore that he had known Harry for twelve years, and that he saw him at 6 am, on Thursday in Gale Lane, Acomb. Harry had requested directions to the Hunt Kennels, but more crucial was Lawson's description of Harry's attire – brown felt hat and overcoat.

'What is your name?' asked Harry.

'Francis Lawson.'

'Well I don't know you.'

Harry Hewitt's appearance was distinctive, even in the dark, with his unkempt hair and wild beard, yet Metcalf could not identify him. Only one tenable piece of evidence linked Harry to the cottage and that was a cuff from the shirt he wore when arrested, found under a cushion on the sofa, but it could have been there for any length of time. When arrested, wearing his billycock and overcoat, two drops of blood were found on his clothes: one on his shirt, the other on his trouser leg. The city analyst, Mr Banes, had studied the evidence from the cottage in detail, including Harry Hewitt's clothing, but he was unable to determine whether the blood was even mammalian, let alone that of the two deceased. The bloodstained axe found at the scene, and discounted as a murder weapon, meant that butchery was carried out at the yard. The blood on Hewitt's clothes could, therefore, have been chicken blood and the analyst was unable to disregard this theory. One final question arose from the evidence and one which the police surgeon made some reference to in his statement. Even though it was apparent that the murderer had washed his hands at the kitchen sink, why did Harry Hewitt have so few traces of blood on his clothing, after committing such a violent slaughter?

On the second day of the inquest, evidence was produced in relation to Harry's identity. In a tin trunk in the bedroom at 5¹/₂ The Crescent, twenty-nine letters had been found. Written in 1890, they began 'Dear Harry' and each related to investigations made by Matthew Stork of Hull, Isabella's brother, concerning Harry's parentage. Cecil Cobb had intended to call Stork into the witness box, but at seventy-four years of age and suffering extreme bronchitis, he was unable to make the journey.

Harry Hewitt was born in 1869 at Bridlington Quay, the son of unmarried Mary Elizabeth Allen. A few months after his birth, she took him to William and Isabella Hewitt to be cared for. Until her death at Collingham in 1877, Mary Allen sent the Hewitt's £5 a quarter for her son's keep. *(Interestingly, Collingham is no more than one and half kilometres from Linton Bridge where Harry was seen on the day of the murder and a footpath runs from the church down the River Wharfe to the bridge.)* From that time until 1883, Mary's brother in law, Mr Beetham of Leigh on Sea, continued with the arrangement, but apart from a few sums paid in 1888, no money had been forthcoming since 1890, by which time Harry had reached twenty-one years of age. The father that Harry claimed lived in London, the cause of his troubles, was unknown.

Though the prosecution had found a possible motive, they had failed to place him in The Crescent on the night of the 28th. There was no evidence to convict him on, not without a shadow of doubt, and his defence thought so too. As the hearing drew to a close, Mr Lucas contended that very point. He asked the bench to consider whether a *Prima Facia* case had been made out; and having made that consideration, discharge his client. No one doubted that the Hewitt's had been murdered. The coroner was convinced it happened about the time that Metcalf had seen the fleeing man. The Magistrates ignored Mr Lucas's plea and informed the jury to consider a verdict.

Harry had not helped himself by his conduct in court, his lack of defence or his appearance. There had been an outcry and the police and coroner were clearly convinced of Harry's guilt. Two of the fifteen-man jury had not been persuaded, but the remaining thirteen had, and they found a case of wilful murder against him. Committed to trial at the next assizes, he was conveyed to Wakefield, to wait for that day.

That day arrived with the opening of the spring assizes at the County Courthouse. Mr Justice Ridley, having breakfasted with the Lord Mayor at the Mansion House, took up his seat on 13 March 1905 and called for the prosecution to begin their case. Mr Milvain KC and Mr Gotrain represented the crown and called as witnesses all those previously heard before the magistrates. Harry's defence was conducted by Messer's Shortt and Godley and was again based upon the fact that no actual evidence directly linked their client to the murder. The case attracted a huge amount of attention from both the public and the press. Once again, Harry's fate was in the hands of a jury.

This time the defence had done their job well. Harry had been groomed and presented a much smarter figure. In fact a witness remarked upon it. When asked if he recognised the accused, John Hobbs said – 'Yes, but you've altered him in some ways a little.'

In summing up, Justice Ridley made it clear to the jury that they could only find Hewitt guilty if they considered him to be so without any reasonable doubt. Whatever anyone thought had taken place in The Crescent, the jury could not say that the prosecution had shown the perpetrator to be Harry Hewitt. Their decision was therefore 'Not Guilty.'

Whoever did murder the Hewitt's; their motive had been other than greed, as William still wore his watch and chain. The case was never reopened; the police considered that they had caught their man.

Harry Hewitt in the dock. (York Evening Press). Author's collection

Chapter 13

A Village Tragedy
Heslington: 1905

On Monday, 11 November 1905, Mr Herbert Daniels, an agent of the Refuge Assurance Company, was around the city making his usual collections. Before wending his way home to 14 Baker Street, he decided to call upon his customers in the little village of Heslington. Just after 4.30 pm, he arrived on the wide main street and made his way through the village for his first call to the Pinkney family. He was certain of a warm welcome from his old friends John and Sarah Pinkney, and their delightful family of five children, former neighbours of his at Aldborough. Going around to the back door of the cottage, he knocked repeatedly but received no reply. Finding the door locked, Daniels called next door at Mary Carr's to inquire if she had seen the family. She had not, but had heard them at 6.30 am; the usual sounds of children crying, the fire grate being raked, Mr Pinkney coughing in the yard – but

14 Baker Street. The Author

Heslington's wide Main Street. The Author

nothing since. The Pinkney's four year old daughter, Eva, had recently been admitted to hospital with an inflamed bladder (rumours of her death had circulated the village all day) and it was possible that they were all out visiting her, but something made Mr Daniels and Mrs Carr proceed. Together, they went to the front door and knocked, once again without reply and this door too was locked; what's more, all the curtains were drawn.

What neither of them knew at the time, was that Sarah Pinkney had asked the local newsagent to call at ten that morning to collect his money and that he had gone away without seeing a soul.

At Mary Carr's insistence, Daniels lifted the sash window and pulled the curtain to one side. Turning pale faced to his companion he said – 'Why missus, there's been murder in the house.'

The Pinkney case would herald a brand of news reporting not seen in the city before. The *Yorkshire Evening Press* was a relative newcomer to the printing presses of York. Founded in 1882, it had already sensationalised stories in the past, but nothing like it did in the winter of 1905. Just over a hundred years earlier when the *Herald* reported the trial of Elizabeth Johnson (Chapter 2) it was speaking to a different class of citizen. Now, with affordable newsprint and increased literacy, the *Yorkshire Evening Press* aimed for a market never before available. It used attention-grabbing headlines and illuminated its stories with bold illustrations. The drawings used to accompany the Pinkney case came in for some strong criticism; many feeling it had gone too far. The York coroner, Mr J W Wood, felt the need to comment on them:

I am not sure that any useful purpose is gained, and it may even be a dangerous practice, because it may suggest to people who are depressed or worried or whose minds are somewhat off the balance, deeds which might not otherwise occur to them.

[Hear, hear, applauded the *Yorkshire Evening Press*]

This view is emphasised by an observation made to me lately by a superintendent of a large lunatic asylum. He said to me that when tragedies like these occur they took great pains to keep the newspapers away from the patients. I am quite sure that if there is such a danger as I have suggested may possibly exist, it only has to be pointed out to the press, and that it will then disappear.

Despite its vicarious methods, the *Evening Press* did deliver the news in a depth previously unseen. Not satisfied with the sanitary proceedings of the coroner's inquest, it sent its reporters, or 'representatives' as it preferred them to be known, out into the streets to interview family, neighbours and

Heslington, circa 1905. The Author

The Pinkney family home. The Author

witnesses, filling its pages with both fact and gossip.

Herbert Daniels would find himself in great demand.

'We'd better get the police,' he told Mary Carr and immediately set out for the village station house. Returning with Constable Farmery, the two men slipped into the cottage through the sash window and found themselves staggered at the sight facing them.

By the door lay John Pinkney, a razor resting at his side, his throat so badly cut that Daniels thought his head nearly severed. On the hearth rug was the body of his wife, Sarah, her head hacked open and weltered in blood. As the men watched in terror, she turned her head towards them, but within minutes had died. Across the room rested the body of little Madge, not yet three years old, so mutilated that she was beyond recognition. The whole dreadful scene was lit by the low light of a burning lamp.

Constable Farmery asked Daniels if there were any more children in the house and being told another three, he made towards the stairs. At that moment, a bundle of rags in Sarah Pinkney's arms moved and the face of five-year-old Arthur peered upwards.

'Please give me something to eat and drink,' he begged.

Daniels lifted him onto a chair and gave him some water. His

The Yorkshire Evening Press *upset the coroner with their depiction of the murder scene.* Author's collection

head was gashed to the bone on both sides and he was missing a thumb and finger on one hand.

'Take me home with you, Mr Daniels,' pleaded Arthur.

Daniels asked him if he knew what had happened, but the boy just shook his damaged head.

'Are you hurting, Arthur?' asked Daniels, and the lad shook his head again.

Leaving the boy alone amid the horror, Daniels and Farmery climbed the stairs in search of the other children. They found them together in the back bedroom. On the bed, dressed only in a shirt, lay the body of eight-year-old John (Jack) Pinkney junior, his face literally cleaved in two. On the floor by the second bed, draped in bedclothes, was the slumped corpse of ten-year-old Elsie. The mattresses and walls bore the stains of the massacre that had been carried out in the tiny room and in it lay the abandoned murder weapon, a hedging billhook, tainted with the blood of an entire family.

Breaking away from the terrible scene in which he stood,

The discovery in the bedroom. Author's collection

Constable Farmery realised that young Arthur needed to get to hospital as soon as possible. He raised the landlord of the *De Yarbrugh Arms*, Mr Kitchen, and had him bring his horse and cart. With Arthur safely on board, he was told to make speed to the city hospital. At the same time, a cycle messenger was dispatched to Dr Stoddart's home in Fishergate, asking that he attend at once.

While on the road to the hospital, Kitchen was making conversation with his travelling companion, Mr Ward, discussing the terrible tragedy they had witnessed. Arthur sat silently between them.

'Was John Pinkney still shepherding, then?' Ward asked Kitchen, but before a reply could be given Arthur suddenly piped up.

'No, he wasn't looking after sheep, he was slashing heads!'

The surgeons found Arthur's skull to be fractured in three places and an immediate operation was carried out. Though he spent the night in a dangerous condition, they thought he would live.

'AWFUL TRAGEDY NEAR YORK,' proclaimed the next days *Yorkshire Evening Press*. 'FAMILY ANNIHILATED,' it shouted, and 'HORRIBLE SCENE OF BLOODSHED.' It was like no other story, and the events played out in that end of terrace cottage had a profound effect on the village of Heslington. In the editorial, we find the *Evening Press* also in more reflective mood:

> *Today the minds of the good people of Heslington and district are occupied pondering over the terrible tragedy in the village yesterday. Never in the annals of the village has there been such an occurrence. The quietude of the street is almost undisturbed today and the visitor to the village would not dream that such a thing as fourfold murder and suicide had been committed only a few hours previously. There is no stir, no morbid crowd in front of the humble dwelling, but the casual passer-by gives more than a cursory glance at the windows, exchanges a word or two with one or other of the neighbours and resumes his journey with his mind concentrated upon the irony of things, and endeavouring to solve the problem of how a peaceable rural family should be victims of a holocaust.*
>
> *Heslington looked drearier than usual today, with its muddy streets and its puddles and the scene of the tragedy looked*

Heslington Manor House. The Author

uninviting with its muddy little garden, well trodden by feet, windows with blinds drawn, and a generally forsaken aspect. An unpretentious room contains the bodies of the dead couple and the three children. Last night the ghastly task of stripping and washing them was carried out and now they lie side by side, murderer and murdered, hacked and disfigured awaiting the inquest, after which they will be laid to rest in their graves.

The coroner's inquest was held the next day. As no public house in the village had a room large enough to cope, the dining room of the Manor House was utilised. The owner, Mr Edward Connell, farmer, butcher and assistant overseer to the General Fire and Life Company, acted as foreman to the jury. The villagers turned out in force to hear the accounts of the drama for themselves.

There was not the slightest doubt as to what had taken place in the Pinkney's cottage. John Pinkney had taken a billhook from the shed, attacked his wife and children, ahead of taking his own life. The purpose of the inquest was, as much as anything, to try and make sense of it all. Why had it happened? With that thought in mind, the first witness was Mr George

Richard Pinkney, a farmer from Flawith, near Easingwold, John's brother.

John Pinkney, he related, had served with the 2nd Battalion West Yorkshire Regiment prior to his discharge on 9 March 1888 due to ill health. He had suffered on several occasions with 'Indian Fever' (Malaria) and his last bout at Moulton in India had curtailed his military career. George Pinkney last saw his bother in late July.

'He came to my house, but I could make nothing of him.'

'Why?' asked the coroner.

'Because he was the worse for drink,' explained George. 'He stayed all night, having missed his train, but left the next morning.'

'Was he in money difficulties, then?'

'Yes, sir.'

'Had he come to you in money difficulties previously?'

'Yes, sir, once.'

'And did you help him?'

'Three years ago I helped him.'

The sources of John's 'money difficulties' were never identified and many witnesses expressed bemusement at his predicament. George Pinkney told the packed room that two weeks ago, John's employer, Mr Charles Dickson of Prospect House, had telegrammed him to say that the bailiffs were in his

Prospect House Farm The Author

brother's home. Charles Dickson had been willing to pay the required thirty-five shillings, if George would act as surety.

'I said that I could not see my way clear to do so as I had lost plenty,' explained George. 'He had had money from me before and never paid me back.'

John had been in the employ of Mr (Alfred) Charles Dickson for nearly five years, shepherd in the winter and general farm labourer in the warmer months. Of late, their working relationship had become strained and on Thursday, 7 November, John had given what his employer described as a 'thorough blackguarding.' Consequently, he was dismissed and given notice to quit his house. However, having made his apologies on Saturday, he was taken back. It would be the last day that Charles Dickson saw him alive and he noticed nothing unusual in his manner.

'What sort of man was Pinkney?' Questioned the coroner.

'A very straightforward man,' replied Dickson. 'And a very conscientious man.'

This view of him was borne out by his neighbours. A private man, who treated his family with great affection, a man whose only character stain seems to have been a quarterly drinking binge upon the arrival of his army pension.

Away from the inquest, a 'representative' of the *Yorkshire Evening Press* interviewed one of John's neighbours, either Richard Moreland, gamekeeper to Lord Deramore, or George Carr, gardener to the same. He learnt more of John's quiet ways, being told how he always seemed to be a good husband, a 'steady man' –

> *But he had been in India as a soldier, and you know what that means. When he gave way to drink, which was perhaps two or three times a year, he behaved in a most peculiar manner, and we gained an insight into his past life that was not altogether of the pleasantest.*

Still seeking answers as to the cause, Dr Stoddart was called, and after hearing him present his findings at the murder scene, Edward Connell asked him –

'Are there not instances of persons running amok who have suffered Indian Fever?'

The three cottages. Left to right – The Morelands, the Carr's and the Pinkney's. The Author

'Oh, yes.'

'There would be a possibility of them doing it after they came to England?'

The doctor's reply was perhaps not what Edward Connell had hoped to hear.

'Personally, I do not think many persons in this country would do it.'

One point bothered the coroner, Mr Wood, above all others. It was the same question that many villagers voiced quietly. How, in such a closely-knit community had it taken so long to discover the crime? He asked Mary Carr if she thought it strange that the family had not been seen all day.

'I didn't think it strange at all,' she said.

'Were the blinds down?'

'Yes, sir.'

'Didn't you think that strange?'

'No, sir,' affirmed Mary. 'Because it had been reported that the child in the hospital had died.'

Mr Wood pushed Mary further than he pushed any other witness. Clearly, he believed that she should have been the one to discover the poor victims earlier in the day and in doing so perhaps save lives.

'Did you knock at the door or go enquire if it was true.'

'No, I never asked anything about it.'

In truth, no one who knew the Pinkney's were sure how long Eva had been in hospital. Only Herbert Daniels could recall that she had been at home when he had called two weeks before. Referring to Mary Carr having heard the family at 6.30 am, but not after, Mr Wood voiced his own feelings.

'It is an extraordinary thing that you didn't hear any further sound.'

'I am quite sure, sir, that I didn't,' Mary Carr told him.

'You could hear almost anything through those walls. Now just think again. Don't you think you heard...'

Mary did not allow him to finish his sentence. She was adamant about her recollection.

'It's no use thinking! I didn't!'

'Have you ever known them all to be in the house in the morning and not come out?' pressed the coroner.

'Yes, sir.'

Edward Connell spoke up at this point, diffusing the situation.

'The husband might have gone to work for ought she knew.'

Mary Carr's husband, George, worked as a gardener for Lord Deramore, and Edward Connell rented the Manor House from him. He could never have allowed Mr Wood to infer that Mary had somehow heard the commotion next door and chosen to ignore it. He had a question of his own to put to her, but her reply may not have been the one he was after.

'When you heard the children cry, were they screaming as if in pain?'

'I didn't take any notice,' Mary answered.

The verdict by the jury that 'John Pinkney murdered his wife and three of his children while in a state of unsound mind before committing suicide' was no surprise. The coroner believed that it had happened at the time when the children had been crying, perhaps having seen their mother felled by the blow of a billhook. Edward Connell, as foreman, was granted the final word:

> *I would like to say, on behalf of my brother jurymen, that we would like to express our deep sympathy with the brother and relatives of the family who have suffered the terrible catastrophe. We deeply regret that such a horrible affair should have taken place in this, our quiet village of Heslington...*

It was a sentiment that ran through the village. Almost a communal feeling of guilt, both that such a tragedy could occur, and that having happened, remain undiscovered for more than ten hours.

The final undertaking was the funeral, and the press coverage encouraged another scene of apparent mass grief. The city had already experienced the funeral of the Hewitt's, when 7,000 turned out to say a sad farewell to total strangers and it happened again in Heslington.

In damp, miserable weather, hundreds tramped the three kilometres from the city to the little village and from all the surrounding villages. They filled the churchyard and lined the main street all the way to the Pinkney's cottage. So large was the crowd that the road became blocked. The buzz of the expectant audience fell silent as the first of the coffins was carried out and placed upon a simple lorry, draped in red baize:

> *Mothers with children in their arms wiped away the falling tear, and even sterner manhood was visibly affected,* wrote the *Yorkshire Evening Press.*

Among the mourners in the church were John Pinkney's brothers, George and Albert, and his three sisters, Mrs Taylor, Mrs Clayton and Mrs Redd. Sarah Pinkney's sisters attended, Miss Barker and Mrs Nay, both from Harrogate.

Following the service, Reverend James Clarke led the coffins to the eastern boundary, where all five Pinkney's would lie in a single grave. This concluding act did not go without incident.

As John's coffin was being lowered, the straps broke and it dropped into the grave. A gasp went around the onlookers and Reverend Clarke paused in his prayers. Two of the bearers hurried back to the church and returned with a ladder. Climbing down, they straightened the coffin and the service continued. With the parents interred side by side, a covering of earth was laid over them

St Paul's church, Heslington. The Author

The Pinkney family – from left to right: John (jr), Eva, John (sr), Arthur, Elsie, Sarah amd Madge. Author's collection

and the children's coffins lowered and set above them. The family said their farewells and then one by one the crowd passed the grave and left...

> *...leaving the dead to sleep in the pretty little churchyard amid the falling autumn leaves.*

The two surviving children, Eva and Arthur, having recovered, went to live with their uncle on the farm at Flawith. The Refuge Assurance Company, though insistent that due to circumstances and payment arrears only a quarter of the sum assured was payable, paid in full at the request of Edward Connell.

We will never know what made a loving father and husband take the life of his wife and children. Financial difficulties prayed on his mind and he worried about Eva in hospital, but perhaps a better clue is provided by the words of his neighbour when he said that when drunk John Pinkney told them of his time in India. 'Not altogether of the pleasantest,' was how he described his memories and the drink revived them. Had the drink and the Indian Fever finally caught up with him?

Chapter 14

The Prevention of Cruelty

Hungate: 1904 and Nether Poppleton: 1908

The country's treatment of its children at work throughout the nineteenth century was harsh in the extreme. Reforms were slow and met with fierce opposition in all quarters. Attempts to improve working conditions prompted some in government to say that free trade would be ruined if children were not put to work. Even lowly chimney sweeps produced convoluted drawings of complex flues in an effort to show how their work would be impossible without the help of small agile boys. So the workshop of the world bought and sold its children like puppies, forced its prized commodity to scramble beneath looms and crawl in the dark like pit ponies. The children of the poor were cheap, dispensable and easily replaceable.

This abuse was apparent, it was carried out in full view, but the cruelty that existed behind closed doors was the secret shame of Victorian England. Those who fought to bring this disgrace out into the open found their path blocked at every turn. Even the great reforming Lord Shaftsbury, was loathed to admit that child abuse was of such a 'private, internal and domestic nature as to be beyond the reach of legislation.' It can only be a source of embarrassment that England had a society for the protection of animals long before it afforded the same protection for its children.

It was a Yorkshire man who began that society. The Reverend Benjamin Waugh was born in Settle and following his theological training at Bradford, took up a position in the east end slums of London. The horror and revulsion that he felt at seeing the abuse that went on, caused him to found the London Society for the Prevention of Cruelty to Children in 1884. Five years of persistent lobbying helped to bring about the so-called Children's Charter of 1889, giving the police the right to enter homes and intervene in suspected cases. It was also the year

that, with Queen Victoria as patron, the London Society became the National Society of Prevention of Cruelty to Children (NSPCC) and 3,947 cases of neglect and abuse brought to the courts nationwide. By 1900, there were 163 uniformed officers or 'cruelty men' and in 1904 the *Prevention of Cruelty to Children Act* gave them the right to take action without the need of police involvement. In excess of one million children had received the Society's help by the end of 1905.

In York, two cases illustrate the society's work, and there was plenty of it. The first is typical; the second is a story that grabbed headlines across the country.

In the April of 1905, Frank Denham, a confectioner's labourer of 1 Bradley's Buildings in Hungate, found himself in the dock at the Police Court. The summons, raised by the NSPCC, claimed that Denham had been neglecting his three children, all under the age of sixteen. Found guilty, he was given three months to improve his behaviour. The society had no desire to remove him from his family; after all he was their breadwinner, even if he had failed them. In July, his conduct was appraised and, unfortunately, Frank Denham returned to court.

Mary Denham took the stand and told her sad tale. Following the earlier reprimand her husband had improved his behaviour. For a whole fortnight, he stopped drinking, went to work and brought food to the table. 'It was wonderful,' she said, but it was too good to last. The drinking started over and he lost his job. Mary Denham was lucky if she was given tuppence a week to feed and clothe the children, if she was given any money at all. She sent the children to her mother and to neighbours in search of food. They were so hungry that they cried for want of a little bread. Mrs Lofthouse, Mary's mother, said – 'I am a poor woman of seventy years of age, and I give to the children because my heart aches for them.'

'Whose fault was that,' asked Mr Norman Crombie, prosecuting on behalf of the NSPCC.

'The father's. He spends his money on drink. The mother and the children are poorly. He never takes food to the house.'

Not quite true, because on 9 July, Denham had taken home sixpence worth of cake and tuppence worth of ham and eaten it in front of the children, despite their obvious need.

Bradley's Buildings in Hungate. The home of the Denham's and Sarah Gamble (see Chapter 9).
York City Libraries

Dr Harry William Reynolds examined the children on two occasions and found them to be suffering from serious neglect. Barely clothed, pale and undernourished, their beds were covered in nothing but strips of stair carpet. Mary Denham, who gave any food she had to her children, was very poorly, weak and unable to care for them properly.

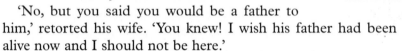

> *It is for the little ones,* she told the court. *I cared not for myself. Before I was ill, I got a bit of bread for my children or they would have been in the grave by now.*

She gave their ages as being eighteen months, three years and thirteen years, but her husband would never have anything to do with the older boy.

Dr Harry William Reynolds Author's collection

'He's not mine,' shouted Denham.

'No, but you said you would be a father to him,' retorted his wife. 'You knew! I wish his father had been alive now and I should not be here.'

Inspector Jackson of the NSPCC had observed the family for nine months and warned the defendant several times about his behaviour. During his numerous visits to the house, he found food on only one occasion – a piece of bread and a little sugar. The parish had been unwilling to help the mother and were it not for himself, neighbours and Dr Reynolds providing food, the children, and most likely the mother, would be dead.

18 St Saviourgate, once home to Dr Reynolds. The Author

Poppleton House. The Author

Frank Denham gave a half-hearted denial of the charges, adding that he would like a separation from his wife so that he would not have to have anything to do with her anymore. Magistrate Mr MacKay sent him to prison for three months with hard labour.

The second case attracted not just the attention of the local press, but also the nationals. During the trial, which lasted three days, journalists wired more than 80,000 words from the post office. York had not seen the likes before. It horrified Edwardian society that a form of Dickensian child neglect, thought to have been left behind in Victorian England could still exist; and under the roof of one of the city's more prominent citizens.

Charles George Golden Rushworth lived at Poppleton House in Nether Poppleton. He was a solicitor and secretary to the York Education Committee, a position that made his conduct even more shocking. He had married, in 1883, Sarah Catherine, the widowed wife of one Captain Scott of Filey, the daughter of a vicar. They had a son in 1886, Cecil, who was, unfortunately, partially sighted and a frail boy. His condition meant that his education was conducted at home, until at the age of sixteen, his parents felt that there was no point in continuing. Cecil would never be strong enough to engage in a professional career, he could not shoot or play cricket; he could not even muster the strength to ride his horse. So in 1903, the Rushworth's decided that a young girl be found.

It was Sarah Rushworth, herself a delicate creature and virtually housebound, who needed the company. Her husband's work meant long unsociable hours and she sat in the large house all alone. If she had a bright, cheery little girl whom she could educate and nurture in return for companionship, then everything would be all right.

Their newspaper advertisement asking for such a girl was answered by Mrs Wilson, a farmer's wife from Westow, between York and Malton. She had replied to an offer of a child some three years previously and paid £10 for the girl named Olive Mabel May. Now aged about eight, the girl was once again available for 'adoption'. Charles Rushworth told Mrs Wilson of his desire for a young girl that he could treat as his own daughter. Arrangements were made, and Olive May sent on approval to Poppleton House to spend time with Sarah Rushworth. She stayed a few days and then retuned to Westow. Five months later an agreement was reached and Olive arrived at York station to be collected by her new 'parents'.

Mrs Wilson described the girl as bright, intelligent and in good health, surely the ideal companion for Sarah Rushworth. Olive was to be the perfect little daughter, who with her teaching, would grow and blossom. They bought her books and blocks of letters, even gave her piano lessons. When she fell ill, they nursed her back to health and gave the very best of foods to bolster her strength. Sarah Rushworth renamed her little girl Nita Smith, though in time she became known simply as 'Smith', just as one might refer to a servant. Things as they were would last less than twelve months.

The Rushworth's kept a manservant, George Thompson, and two maids, but during 1904, one of the maids died and the other was dismissed. They were not replaced, indeed, other than Thompson; the Rushworth's had trouble keeping staff for any length of time. Cecil Rushworth, totally devoted to his mother, became cook and poor Olive, the scullery maid. Her 'mother' had decided that she was incapable of benefiting from education. The only thing stopping the Rushworth's from sending Olive to the workhouse was their kindly nature – for it was certainly considered.

Olive May had been in the village of Nether Poppleton for almost a year when William Hayes pictured these children running close to the gates of Poppleton House.
Author's collection

What was to be done? The answer came in early 1905 when the Rushworth's spied little Dora Crees in Hull. The girl's mother came from Stonehouse in Devon, but it so happened that she was living in Hull at that time. A correspondence was entered into and the Rushworth's eventually managed to convince her of their good intentions. Namely, that her daughter would benefit from the advantages of living at Poppleton House and all it had to offer. Ten-year-old Dora was handed over on 6 July at York station.

Just like Olive, she was initially treated with affection, although at her 'sister's' expense. Olive's good clothes were handed to Dora, and Olive made to wear garments cut from old army blankets. She went without underwear and made to sleep in the kitchen on a straw filled sack with the family's beloved dogs, Fiff and Belia. The excuse given was that she was unable to control her bladder. Her habits, said Sarah Rushworth, were filthy. Dora slept in Cecil's room on Olive's old bed, divided from the young man by a curtain.

In a short space of time, Dora became just as ill-treated. She was physically punished, often with a whip, and made in turn to punish Olive. Both girls were regularly left without food and when it was given it was frequently inedible. Olive even took to scavenging from the pig tub.

In such a small village, rumours spread quickly and the strange goings on at Poppleton House were rich sources of gossip. Who were the little girls? Why did no one see them around the village? They did not attend church, school nor join with other children at play. One person who did see them was the postman, Samuel Standish, but when he spotted them they ran away. If he happened to see them stood on the balcony they would quickly lay flat out of sight.

'They were afraid of me, ' he said. 'I don't know why they should be.'

Standish never questioned their fear of him and yet claimed to have witnessed their miserable condition, even noticing scars on Olive. For whatever reason, he did not report the Rushworth's. But then why should he? Mr Rushworth was an important gentleman, far and above any suspicions Sam Standish might have harboured.

Matters reached a head in 1907. Just how the NSPCC got to hear of Dora and Olive is unclear. It may have been one of two men, John Leaf and Arthur Long, or possibly as a result of a letter written by Dora to her mother telling her what was happening. It may also have been the case that the rumours had spread beyond Nether Poppleton.

At the start of that year, George Thompson, the coachman, left the Rushworth's employ after twenty years of service. A relief to the girls because they alleged that he beat them with as much severity as Mrs Rushworth. John Leaf replaced him on 11 March and he was to witness first hand the treatment endured by the girls. Leaf saw Olive digging in the bins for food, sleeping naked on her straw bed, even on one occasion finding her stood in the kitchen, in his words, 'like a stuck sheep,' and bleeding profusely. Sarah Rushworth told him that 'Smith' had cut herself on some broken crockery. When he suggested a doctor, Mrs Rushworth dismissed the notion – 'She will be all right directly.'

Leaf, during his morning runs to town with Charles

Arthur Long saw Olive sat on the doorstep, shivering with cold. The Author

Rushworth, told his master of the things he had seen. Rushworth chose to disbelieve, or ignore, his coachman. He was a busy man. Mrs Rushworth ran the house and he would no more interfere in it than she would in his office.

And so the abuse continued until the autumn.

On 2 October, Arthur Long, a neighbour of the Rushworth's, stood in his backyard, looking into the garden of Poppleton House. It was a cold, frosty Sunday morning, the time was between 9.30 am and 10.30 am. Despite living in the house for six months, he saw something he had never seen in all that time. It was a girl, sat on the front doorstep, crying and shivering. Long could see how terrible she was. Her feet and legs were bare, begrimed in dirt. Her dress was shabby and badly made. As he watched, Mrs Rushworth came out of the front door.

'You've been out since half past eight doing these steps,' she scolded. 'I will make you finish them.'

With that she slapped Olive hard about the face.

'Oh dear,' whimpered the girl, and Long could see how weak and helpless she was. The NSPCC would later claim that those few hours spent trembling with cold on the steps was the longest

Part of Bishophill Senior, where Helen Bennington ran her rescue home, previously the Refuge for Fallen Women. The Author

period of time that Olive spent outside in five years.

On 28 November, Olive and Dora's misery at Nether Poppleton ended. As a consequence of information received, he would say no more, Inspector James Campbell of the NSPCC called at the Rushworth's home. Mrs Rushworth was on one of her regular trips to Scarborough. John Leaf, who had not driven Charles Rushworth to work that morning, admitted the Inspector and called Olive from the kitchen. Campbell saw her for the first time – pale, dirty, undernourished and altogether a wretched picture of childhood. Her clothing was threadbare and she wore a large odd pair of men's boots on her tiny feet.

He listened to the girls' account of their ordeal and then removed them from the house, taking them to Mrs Bennington at the York Rescue Home in Bishophill, commonly called The Shelter. Two eminent doctors examined the girls, Dr Draper and the campaigning Dr W A Evelyn. They found both of them to be seriously underweight and bearing the scars of past wounds.

Dora, who was bright and quick, had certainly suffered, but it was Olive's condition that caused most alarm. Weighing only thirty-two kilos, she was enuric, anaemic and totally illiterate in every way. One scar alone was eighteen centimetres long by thirteen centimetres wide, which Olive told them had been caused by a flat iron. Another scar near her mouth was the result of having had a hot poker pressed to her face and evidence of the 'dog whip' was abundant.

Charles Rushworth was furious, if not a little worried. He reprimanded his coachman for allowing the inspector access to the girls, but Leaf maintained that he had no choice. Rushworth, knowing that a court case was imminent, offered Leaf £10 if he could 'put a stop to all of this.' This amounted to six months wages and was an obvious bribe to make sure that he appeared for the defence. John Leaf knew too much. He managed to stay at Poppleton House until December, when he was dismissed with a week's pay.

There was no way of avoiding a court case. Charles Rushworth suggested to his solicitor, ex-Lord Mayor of York, Vernon Wragge, that a payment of £100 each to Olive and Dora would make it go away, but it would have been money wasted. The NSPCC fully intended to press charges. This was no beer soaked labourer from Hungate abusing his children; this was a family man of some standing engaging in 'white-slavery.' The man whose function it was to ensure that each child in the city got an education had deprived two children in his care of that very thing.

The case came to court in January 1908. Mindful of hostile feelings on both sides, the NSPCC had the case investigated by its London branch and outside counsel was sought to front its team of prosecutors. The Rushworth's took the decision to forego a jury and be tried summarily, that is by the magistrates. Charles Rushworth would, therefore, enter the court among his peers and legal brethren. He could not take the chance of facing a jury filled with concerned parents; much less have Olive and Dora do the same. He would take his chances with Sir John Grant Lawson MP (Chairman), Colonel Wilkinson, Mr Richard Lawson and Major Allenby, all four observed by Lord Deramore. The prosecution was handled by Mr Clarke Hall on behalf of George Crombie and Sons of 46 Stonegate, York, while

Little Betty's Cafe at 46 Stonegate was previously the office of Norman Crombie, solicitor to the NSPCC. The Author

the Rushworth's employed the services of Mr Kemp KC and the renowned Mr H Vernon Wragge. Both Charles and Sarah Rushworth were charged under the *Prevention of Cruelty to Children Act*, in that they had in their custody, children under the age of sixteen whom they did wilfully ill-treat and neglect. A further charge was laid against Mrs Rushworth in respect of Olive May's excessive treatment.

During the course of the trial, the Rushworth's ran the gauntlet of the mob that gathered outside the courthouse and their home. In Nether Poppleton their return each evening was heralded by a 'Tin Pot Band' playing rough music. This custom, prevalent in the nineteenth century, particularly in East Yorkshire, was intended to drive undesirables out of their homes. A motley collection of musical instruments, usually pots and pans (in this case it included a couple of battered bugles) would be drummed haphazardly. Sometimes, in the related custom known as 'Riding the Stang,' an effigy of the person would be paraded in front of the band on a board or ladder before being burnt. This bad feeling caused two defence witnesses to flee. Former employee, George Thompson and his wife, left York for Harrogate with absolutely no intention of returning. Their loss was felt.

The stories told in court shocked the city. Each scar on Olive's frail body told a scandalous tale. How her hand had been plunged into boiling water, her face and leg branded with a poker, her thigh burnt with an iron. Dora, who made an excellent witness, told of their beatings with the 'dog whip,' a cane with several leather cords attached to the end and how Mrs Rushworth doused Olive in water and then reprimanded her for making such a mess.

The defence questioned the medical evidence, as they tried to convince the magistrates that the girls' injuries could have been caused before their arrival at Poppleton House. However, Dr Draper and Dr Evelyn were more than sure of their findings. They had no doubt that the visible injuries were consistent with the explanations given by Olive and Dora. What's more, Olive's enurism had cleared while staying at The Shelter and she did not appear as anaemic as she had been when admitted. The curvature of her spine, in their view, had been exacerbated by her harsh treatment.

Sarah Rushworth's demeanour throughout did not help her case. She appeared not to know why she was in court at all. The whole episode was an unnecessary imposition. Letters written by Dora to her at Scarborough were introduced to show that all had been well in the home:

Dear Mistress,

I am writing hoping you and Master Cecil are well. The little mother hen is dead. George brought her into the house and did the best he could for her. Thank you very much for the sweets you sent me. I think it would be better for you to wait until spring to get a new dress; if you get a black one you would not like it. The little dogs are not well yet. The horses are well. I hope the weather is fine; it is fine here, but the wind is nasty. I shall be glad when I get older to be able to go with you. I will now close my letter with love.
D. CREES.

'So she sent you sweets from Scarborough,' asked Mr Kemp. 'Yes,' replied Dora. 'She sent some to both of us.'

'Is that the kind of letter a child is likely to send to a woman who is badly treating her?' Kemp enquired of the magistrates. 'Can you explain that?' he asked Dora.

She could not answer his question, but the prosecution produced further letters to show that Sarah Rushworth had written to Dora reproaching her for failing to write with news of home. She also made Dora write to her mother in Devon, telling of how life was good at York. Finally in November 1907, the little girl had plucked up enough courage to let her mother know the truth. Sarah Rushworth had attempted to countermand this letter by writing to Mrs Crees, explaining that Dora was under the mischievous influence of 'Smith'. Some felt that Dora's letter to her mother was passed to the NSPCC, thereby beginning the investigation. Yet for many in the city, the hero of the hour was John Leaf. Dr Evelyn certainly thought so and he applauded his actions in a letter to the editor of the *Yorkshire Herald* on 13 January:

> Sir – Had it not been for the man Leaf those two poor children might still be in the shackles of their 'white slavery'. Cannot something be done to show everyone's appreciation of his conduct, and to encourage others to do the same under similar circumstances? – Yours Faithfully,
> W A Evelyn M D
>
> P.S. – Subscribers may rest assured that every care will be taken to see that the money is properly applied.

The defence knew what a key witness Leaf was and tried to sully his reputation, claiming that he was a drunkard. Sarah Rushworth even declared that if there had been abuse upon the girls, then it had not begun until Leaf's arrival in their home. She would have to be careful, because either there had or had not been abuse, and her defence was claiming that there had not been any at all. Leaf proved to be a good witness. He stuck to his story under cross-examination. He never denied liking the odd drink, neither did he deny taking 'the pledge' when asked by Charles Rushworth to do so, but John Leaf would have agreed to most things if it meant keeping his job. When he took up the position with the family in March 1908, he had been a broken man, recently separated from his wife and children. The landlord of the Lord Nelson in Nether Poppleton wrote to the *Herald*:

Sir – With regard to the statement made by Mr Kemp concerning Mr Leaf and his drinking habits at a public house in Poppleton owned by a Mr Eastwood, I beg leave to differ in my opinion with same, as said Mr Leaf never visited my house on more than two occasions when in the employ of Mr Rushworth, and I can safely say that I have never seen him worse for liquor, and why my name should be brought into this case passes comprehension. Yours,
P. EASTWOOD.

Poppleton, January 10th, 1908.

Mr Eastwood's Lord Nelson, *the infrequent watering hole of John Leaf.* The Author

Though Charles Rushworth maintained that Leaf was dismissed because of his drunkenness, it was clear that this principle witness for the prosecution could not remain under the same roof. Just prior to his discharge, Leaf received a letter from Sarah Rushworth and her son. Cecil wrote – 'You have often seen Dora hit Olive with brushes and kicked her as well.' Sarah Rushworth added:

> *Dear John, Smith never slept in the kitchen, she was hit by no one but Dora. I never touched her and know that you never did. She had plenty of bedding. The letter ended with the words – You can burn this.*

Cecil Rushworth remained devoted to his mother during the trial. He would have said anything to help her, including trying to accuse John Leaf of treating the girls like wretched dogs.

'I would not give such a beast house room,' Leaf is meant to have said.

'Have you seen a good deal of these children?' Mr Hall asked Cecil.

'Yes,' he replied.

'You know the circumstances under which they came to your house?'

'Yes.'

'You knew the position these children were to occupy in the house?'

Cecil preferred not to answer that particular question.

'Were you to look upon them as sisters?' Mr Hall enquired.

'No. I did not regard them as such.'

'Did you regard them as household drudges?'

Once again, Cecil thought it best to remain silent.

'Did you have any chivalry towards the girls?'

Silence.

'Do you know what chivalry means?'

'No,' admitted Cecil.

Charles Rushworth's defence was a simple one. He knew nothing. He had never seen the girls mistreated; he had not noticed their disgraceful appearance. He was a busy man and household affairs were the concern of Mrs Rushworth, although he did, when questioned, admit that Olive looked much healthier than when he had last seen her. But it was the question of the girls' education that concerned Mr Hall. How had a man who served on the board of the education committee, a man who sought to punish those whose children did not attend school, allowed the same to take place under his own roof?

'Even in the case of a mentally defective child,' stated Mr Hall: 'It was the duty of the guardian to see that they are well educated. Was no effort made with regard to this child?'

'No, she was neither epileptic nor mentally defective. Her

York House on Clifford Street housed the offices of the Education Committee. The Author

habits made her such that she would not have been received at school,' answered Rushworth.

'Is that seriously the only answer you give the question?'

Charles Rushworth told the court that he judged Olive only fit for a babies class and yet she had been eleven years of age when she came to him. (Mrs Wilson had thought her to be about eight years old.) Finding a suitable school would have been very difficult. Mr Hall wanted to know if Rushworth considered it an important duty of parents to have their children educated.

'I should say so... in ordinary cases,' was Rushworth's measured reply.

'And if other people fail to take those steps would you think it right to take proceedings against them?'

Charles Rushworth allowed the laughter in the courtroom to die down before answering.

'I should take into account all the circumstances of the case.'

The magistrates certainly took notice of the circumstances. They found Charles George Golden Rushworth guilty of cruelty, but only by association, because as head of the household he was responsible for his wife's actions. They imposed the full statutory penalty of £50 plus costs. His life as a solicitor was over and he was later dismissed from the York Education Committee. He was fortunate in that the board felt that his pension of £150 per annum could not be withheld. He would never again hold his head high among the city's elite society.

Sarah Rushworth was considered the main offender. Her sentence would be six months in respect of her cruelty towards Olive and three months for the treatment of Dora. It was the minimum allowed by law - 'Too lenient,' was the general feeling. Suppressing a sob, she rose and said – 'My son wishes to go to prison with me.' Sir John calmly informed her that this would not be possible. The next nine months of her life would be spent in Armley Gaol.

During the trial, her sanity had been called into question, rumours circulated of her having once been a spy in Paris and George Beedham of Stamford Bridge asked the editor of the *Yorkshire Herald* if she was not the same widow of Captain Scott who was found guilty of an act of cruelty towards a servant in

Pocklington a generation ago.

On the evening of 13 January 1908, a crowd gathered on platform No 2 at York station to see Mrs Rushworth depart for gaol. A good many of them missed her, as they mistakenly believed she was bound for Wakefield. As 7 pm approached, a procession of NER police officers sealed off platform No 4 and the prisoner was swiftly placed in a 3rd class carriage. In Leeds,

A crowd gathered at York Railway Station as Sarah Rushworth set out for Armley Gaol. The Author

a good size crowd had amassed on the platform and outside the station, and though the police did their best to protect their charge, one woman managed to strike the disgraced Sarah Rushworth with the point of an umbrella.

'You bitch!' she screamed. 'I'd like to burn you, as you burnt the children.'

So what of the children? In a letter to the *Herald*, Mrs Helen Bennington of the York Rescue Home made an appeal:

> ...*Dora Crees has gone home to her mother's care, but the poor little Olive, who had far the worst treatment, has no mother, no home, no money, no clothes and no one who really has any responsibility.*
> *Yet are there not numbers of warm-hearted Yorkshire souls who will try, even late in the day, to blot out the memory of those dark deeds of cruelty practiced on this poor waif of humanity?*

The NSPCC seeks out sad cases, and justly so thought Mrs Bennington, but people must not forget that the York Shelter and establishments like it were left to pick up the pieces.

The *Yorkshire Herald*, who displayed a certain amount of sympathy for the Rushworth's, feeling that their sentences were 'stern but just,' ended its editorial round up of the case with this caution:

> *It is hoped that the result of the trial will act as a warning to those who undertake the care or secure the services of young people, because flagrant and shocking as this case is, we believe there are thousands of cases of barbarity and cruelty, equally as bad or worse, that are not found out, because the cruelty is inflicted by parents and not by guardians.*

Chapter 15

Almost Death by Chocolate

Huntington: 1920

At midday on 7 April 1919, two men alighted from the Durham train at York Station. Making their way to a nearby busy public house, they met with another man as arranged. He produced a document, which the two men witnessed; not to the signature of the man, but to that of a woman neither man had ever met. Having been thoroughly rehearsed as to the details of the story, they caught the 6.30 pm train back to Durham, arriving home in Fencehouses at 9 pm. In the pocket of one of the men, was the last will and testament of Annie Holmes of Fern Cottage, Huntington.

The city of York evokes many images – the railway, the Minster, the river, the racecourse, the old city walls – fitting then, that our next tale involves its most famous export, chocolate.

Annie Holmes had grown up in Durham. Her family, the Liddle's, were a county family, good farming stock and well known. She married Francis Holmes, also a farmer, and they

York Railway Station – once the largest in Europe. The Author

Huntington, circa 1919. The Author

moved to a property on the rich Suffolk soil. Sadly, things did not go according to plan and in May 1917, the couple were forced to sell the farm and head back north.

Annie's brother, Thomas, was a successful gentleman farmer. He owned land near Durham, York and Market Weighton and it was to his farm at Thornton le Clay, north of York, that Annie and Francis came to live.

Thomas Liddle and Francis Holmes were not the best of friends. Thomas could not bring himself to find acceptance for the man whom he considered unsuitable as a husband for a

Liddle. The friction between them grew to such a height that Annie, leaping to her husband's defence, fell out with her brother. Francis had managed to find a property in Huntington – Fern Cottage – but it required some work before they could move in. Unable to stay a moment longer with Thomas, the couple rented a house in nearby Flaxton and moved into Fern Cottage in the autumn of 1918.

The time that Annie spent in Huntington would be unfortunately brief. She was ill; indeed, Annie knew that she was dying. This knowledge prompted her to write to her brother, despite her husband's objections:

> *Dear Tom,*
> *Just a line to say I am very bad. Come to me at once.*
> *Your loving sister,*
> *Annie Holmes.*

She sent the letter in early January 1919. It went unanswered

Fern Cottage. The adjoining farm has long since vanished.. The Author

Clematis House, Huntington. The Author

and so a second was sent, very similar to the first, but this too went without reply.

Annie's condition worsened and so a long-standing friend of some thirty years was taken on as help in the cottage. Miss Annie Hardy of Clematis House, spent many hours in the company of her friend, caring for her while she watched her become bedridden and moving ever closer to the end. That day came on 13 April 1919 and it began a series of events that would end in the courtrooms.

Francis had no desire to see Thomas at the funeral, but he attended. He had learnt of his sister's death through family friends. They avoided one another and the day passed without incident. Two days after the funeral, Thomas called to see Mary Walker, a friend of Annie's. Mary lived at 55 Stonegate, the wife of a jeweller, Robert Walker, and together they had witnessed Annie's will in early April. Thomas was keen to ascertain the date of that will. Mary could not remember, but between them, they arrived at 2 April being the most likely.

'Did you read the will?' asked Thomas. Mary said that she had not. 'You should have done, ' said Thomas, adding, 'but there is another will and there'll be some bother about it.'

This other will, had been delivered by post to Thomas on the 23 April; sent by Arthur Oliver of Fencehouses in County Durham. Save for £300 of smaller donations, the bulk of Annie's estate, some £1,000 had been left to Thomas – not a penny to her husband. Francis was furious; how could his wife do this? Why leave it to Thomas Liddle? She had made her last will on 2 April and now here was Thomas claiming that another was made less than a week later. It had to be a forgery, and Thomas was right, there was going to be some bother.

Arguments raged between the two men for months, accusation and counter accusation, each claiming the love of Annie for themselves, each claiming to hold her last true will and testament. Finally, Francis involved the police in late 1919. They interviewed Thomas Liddle about the accusation and he supplied them with all the answers.

In January of that year, he had visited his sister at Fern Cottage at her request. They had never really fallen out, the problem had been her husband who had done his utmost to keep them apart. On that January day, Annie had been alone in the house. She had wanted it that way, because there was a task

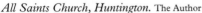

All Saints Church, Huntington. The Author

to perform and she trusted only him. Annie feared that Miss Annie Hardy, under the guise of carer, was secretly planning to make herself mistress of Fern Cottage upon her death.

They sat at a table and Annie dictated her will to him. She was so weak that she found it difficult to write and afterwards the strain of it all forced her to bed, where she placed the will beneath her pillow. This was the last he saw of it, until it arrived by post from Durham following his sister's sad demise. It was hardly his fault that Annie had chosen to leave her good-for-nothing husband, precisely nothing.

The police headed north to Fencehouses to interview colliery workers, Arthur Oliver and Joseph Dawson, witnesses to the contested document.

Oliver had known Thomas Liddle as a boy, though they were not lifelong friends. During his time in France, where he had served his country between 1914 and 1917, Annie had written to him on several occasions, for no other reason than their families knew each other. They were letters of support for a young man caught up in the horrors of war. He claimed, that because of this kind gesture he had always wished to see her and say thank you. After Dawson's sister received a letter on 6 April telling of Annie's illness, he resolved to visit.

Oliver and Dawson, spruced up in their Sunday suits, arrived in York at midday on 7 April. From there, they made immediately for Huntington, stopping only in the village to ask directions from a small boy. Miss Hardy answered the door and having established the purpose of their visit, showed them through to Annie's bedroom. She was then asked to go away, leaving Annie alone with two virtual strangers. True, the men were known to her, but she had never met them and must have wondered why they were there. Apparently not, as the following transaction would seemingly illustrate.

During their conversation, Annie produced some papers from beneath her pillow. It was a will and she asked Oliver and Dawson to witness the signature. Her hand was frail and Arthur Oliver had to hold it steady while she signed her name and dated it. Once the men had put their names to it, Annie asked Oliver to keep it safe and upon news of her death, send it to her bother. A fortnight later, he had done just that.

Joseph Dawson's telling of the story matched that of his friend word for word and both men could describe in detail the interior of Fern Cottage. They also provided a very good description of Miss Annie Hardy, which was quite a feat of memory, as she had never seen them. Indeed, nobody saw them, arriving or leaving, they came and went in apparent secrecy.

Clearly, all was not as it seemed and a charge of forgery was brought against Liddle, Oliver and Arthur at the spring assizes of 1920. At the time of his arrest, Thomas said – 'It is all silly, it is all just silly.'

It was a simple case, which was to attract little attention, a Middlesbrough murder taking the headlines. Mr Lowenthal for the prosecution attempted to show that Oliver and Dawson were never at Fern Cottage at any time and that the will of Annie Holmes was the work of Thomas Liddle.

He produced William Rust, the manager of Barclays Bank, who gave testimony as to the signature on the suspect document. Though there was some resemblance to Annie's script, in his opinion it was not hers. Also called was Annie's solicitor, Ernest Ralph Dodsworth, of Gray and Dodsworth in Duncombe Place, York. He had drawn up the will dated 2 April, witnessed by Robert and Mary Walker, and he was of no doubt that the signature on the alleged forgery was itself counterfeit.

Miss Annie Hardy, now Mrs Thompson, having married Huntington gardener, John Raper Thompson, stood in court and told how she was at Fern Cottage for the whole of 7 April and at no time did Oliver and Dawson visit. Close neighbour, Mrs Lund, had sat at her window on the afternoon in question and did not see the two men either. Mr Waugh, for the defence, intercepted her testimony – 'They may have seen you, though you did not see them.'

Hannah Jackson, Francis Holmes' sister, contested Thomas's claim to have been at Fern Cottage in January as she had been there herself for the whole of that month, without seeing him. Sister and brother stated that March was the earliest he could have made his visit. Moreover, neither Hannah Jackson nor Miss Hardy had ever found anything beneath her pillow and Annie was more than capable of writing her own will in January without the need for dictation. In fact, she had written her own on 2 April.

Barclays Bank at the corner of Pavement and Parliament Street. The Author

The final witness for the prosecution was James Davidson from the payroll offices of Lambton colliery. He produced records to show that Joseph Dawson had been at work on 7 April. Dawson denied the evidence, saying that he had been absent from his work for a fortnight around that time with an injury to his arm. The defence pointed out that it was common practice to get a work colleague to clock an absentee in, to avoid loss of earnings, but colliery foreman, William Knox, was also adamant that Dawson worked on that day.

For the defence, Mr Waugh brought to court, Ernest Parkin, booking clerk at Durham railway station. On the morning of 7 April, he had indeed issued two third class return tickets to York. They were the only ones to that destination he had sold, but he could not confirm that it was Oliver and Dawson who had obtained them.

Waugh struggled to produce any firm evidence of the accused having been in Huntington and the handwriting certainly pointed towards Thomas Liddle having forged his sister's will. His only ploy was to discredit Francis Holmes, making it seem as though the feud between brother and sister was entirely of his own making, if not his imagination. However, the grieving widower had the protection of the judge, who quashed Waugh's attempts.

The jury returned a decision of guilty on the three men, but sentencing was deferred for a later date. With Mr Lowenthal's prediction of a five-year prison sentence ringing in his ears, Thomas Liddle hatched a plan of revenge. Unfortunately, he would apply as much forethought to this scheme as his last.

On 11 April 1920, he left his Market Weighton farm for Pocklington, where he made himself very noticeable to all that he could. This was very important, because at midday when he sneaked away on a train to York, he required witnesses who would swear that he had been about the town all day.

He carried with him seven small parcels, each wrapped in a telegram form. Knowing that his handwriting could be identified, Liddle addressed each packet in a style different to his own (a ruse that would fail him). Posting them in York, he returned to Pocklington and from there back home, where his wife, Mary Ann, awaited.

On 13 April, a parcel arrived at the Stonegate home of jeweller, Robert Walker, the home he shared with his wife Mary and sister, Margaret. Opening the parcel he found three chocolates and a message which read – 'Your Easter egg. One of each.' There appeared to be no clue as to the sender, and so rightly suspicious Mr Walker tossed the gift into the dustbin.

Stonegate before the tourists arrive. The Author

At the same time, similar parcels arrived with solicitor, Ernest Dodsworth, William Rust at Barclays Bank and John Raper and Annie Thompson in Huntington. A further two packages arrived at 7 Brierville, Durham, the home of Hannah Jackson and, at the time of the trial in March, her brother Francis, who had since returned to Fern Cottage. She unwrapped hers to find, along with the chocolates, the message – 'Daddy's Easter egg, with love.'

When John Raper Thompson opened his parcel, he found three chocolates and the words – 'Happy Easter,' written on a scrap of paper. After his lunch, John ate one of the chocolates and as he did so, noticed a strange taste. Annie Thompson placed one against her tongue, but finding the same peculiar flavour, threw it away. John returned to his work, but inside half an hour fell seriously ill and rushed into hospital. He came close to losing his life. Had he eaten the chocolate on an empty stomach, then he would most certainly have died, as it was, it took him several months to fully recover. His symptoms bore all the hallmarks of strychnine poisoning.

Alerted to John's distress, William Rust and Ernest Dodsworth sent their chocolates to George Grinling, analytical chemist with Rowntrees. He found traces of what he believed to be strychnine and so sent them to the city analyst, John Evans.

In one of Ralph Dodsworth's chocolates, he found 0.25 of a grain, while two of William Rust's each contained 0.51 of a grain. The medical dosage would have been 0.0625 of a single grain. These Easter gifts were more than capable of killing.

The police made straight for Market Weighton. Thomas Liddle vehemently denied the accusation, but in his office, they found a tin containing rotten meat laced with strychnine, a bundle of telegram forms hanging from a nail and in his jacket,

Gray and Dodsworth had their offices in the former Dispensary, close to the Minster in Duncombe Place. The Author

a postcard bearing the memorandum – 'Chocolates.' He claimed that his niece had asked for some and that the postcard was a reminder, but neither the police nor the jury believed him.

At the summer assizes of July 1920, Thomas Liddle was found guilty of endangering the life of John Raper Thompson. When Mr Justice Shearman addressed the court, it was packed with ladies of the city, eager for a view of the poisoner who had wronged his own sister.

In the case of conspiracy against Arthur Oliver and Joseph Dawson, he set the prison term at eighteen months. Oliver had presented a letter to the court setting out the true story, and this helped to influence a more lenient sentence:

> *Although I am sorry for them, said Shearman. They will each go to prison for eighteen months, but having regard to their previous characters, I do not add hard labour.*

The two men were removed and Liddle brought into the dock. On the charge of the forged will, Shearman sentenced him to five years in prison, but a sterner sentence awaited the fifty-nine year old farmer:

> *...I have to treat this verdict, as connected with the other facts of the case, as an attempt to injure by poison half a dozen respectable witnesses, whose characters have been attacked in court... This is as serious a thing in a peaceful country as any person can do. For that I sentence him to ten years penal servitude. It will run concurrent with the other.*

To that punishment, Justice Shearman added hard labour, a frightening prospect to a man of Liddle's years. On top of this, he made it clear that the costs of both cases would be the highest allowed and met by Liddle alone.

'I am quite innocent, sir,' said Liddle before he was taken down. 'Not Guilty.'

There is a footnote to the story. Ralph Dodsworth's son, Benjamin, took over his father's practice and went on to serve the city of York as Under Sheriff. It was many years after the case of the poisoned chocolates, whilst Benjamin was carrying out his duty of summoning jurors at the Leeds Assizes that he saw, much to his surprise, sat in the jurors box, Mr Thomas Liddle.

Chapter 16

Who Killed Norma Dale?

Tang Hall: 1946

In 1946, Britain was emerging from the long dark night of World War Two. There was new hope. In the 'Britain Can Make It' exhibition in London, manufacturers displayed such wondrous goods as portable radios, no bigger than cameras; heated beds; a bicycle with a recharging electric motor; shoes made of clear plastic, like Cinderella's glass slipper and clothes fashioned from brightly coloured cloth, that seemed to sweep away the dowdy war years.

It was the year that saw the formation of the York Civic Trust, the body empowered with the conservation of the historic city and the cultural and social well being of its citizens. Like all towns in Britain, it was a time of change. A time to rebuild.

Norma Dale is a pretty, cheerful little girl, fast approaching her fifth birthday. She has light brown hair, big eyes and bright rosy cheeks. On that September morning she is returning from her tap dancing lessons in Holgate Road, accompanied by her mother. She has recently started school and teachers describe her as an intelligent child, quick and eager to learn. She has a loving family, and Norma Dale, age four years and ten months, has nothing to fear.

Rawdon Avenue. The Author

The family home is on Rawdon Avenue in the Tang Hall district, an area of post-World War One development on the eastern fringes of the city. Cyril and Frances Dale have three children and Norma is the youngest. They are well known in the neighbourhood. Cyril once played Rugby League for the York team and now coaches at the Heworth Club. An everyday family, living an everyday life in a bright new world.

When mother and daughter arrived home, they found a fish and chip lunch waiting for them. Norma couldn't finish her chips; some biscuits and fruit given by an Aunt earlier that day had taken the edge off her appetite. She sat for a while drawing and her father did a sketch of a pram for her. Then he went out with a friend to see a local rugby game.

Norma was a lively child and she gave up drawing, dashing in and out of the house in the hope of seeing some playmates. She had on a white summer dress, white socks and smart black and red leather strap shoes. At around 2.40 pm she popped into the house again and her mother gave her a rice cake before she skittled away once more. Frances Dale got changed to out again and at 3.00 pm went into the street to shout for her daughter. But there was no sign of little Norma.

She walked the streets, calling for her daughter, knowing even then that something was wrong. Norma didn't wander away from home, neither was she likely to have walked off with a stranger. Very soon, neighbours came out to help and word soon got around that Norma Dale was missing. There was a large search group already scouring the estate when Cyril Dale arrived home to hear the awful news. The search went on until midnight, for parents and police it went on through the night. They looked everywhere – in sheds, in outhouses, in gardens and through the waste ground at the rear of Rawdon Avenue where the children loved to play around the beck that ran through it. At 11 pm a broadcast was made on the City Relay System, asking for information – but there was nothing.

The morning of the 22nd came without any news and the distraught family had exhausted their efforts. There was nowhere left to look.

Eleven-year-old Michael Duffy should have been in church but he was 'jigging it'down at the beck. Dressed in his 'Sunday

The corner of the wasteland at the rear of Rawdon Avenue where Norma Dale's body lay. The Author

Best' he made his way across the rough ground, a young boy enjoying his unexpected freedom in the late summer sunshine. He could see a coal lorry, belonging to a local resident, parked up on the waste land and as he walked nearer, something laid in the grass close by it. He realised at once that this was Norma, it was her white silky dress and his first thought was that she was resting. Then he saw that one of her shoes was missing and that her face was blue. Michael Duffy turned and ran for all he was worth to the Dale's house to deliver the awful news. Back at his own home, two doors away, his father clipped his ears for making up such terrible lies. It was 10.30 am and Cyril Dale carried his daughter's body back home, a distance of fifty-four metres and the police were called.

Superintendent Cyril Carter and Inspector Thomas Capstick, Head of CID, handled the investigation. Their first job was to place a large doll in the position where the body was found and seal the area off. One fact seemed apparent very quickly. Norma's body had not lain there through the night. The strip of ground, often used as a rubbish dump, had been extensively searched and many neighbours had looked from their bedroom windows and gardens across it that very morning. The body had not been hidden, it could be easily seen, and indeed one man had walked by the spot earlier.

Ex-soldier, Fred Glover, lived five doors away from the Dale house. He stated that only ten minutes before the discovery, he had gone to his coal lorry to get some petrol, which he was going to use to clean some clothes and he had seen nothing. The body was found not two metres from his vehicle and he could not have failed to see it. This being the case, somebody had dumped Norma's body between 10.15 am and 10.30 am, strengthening the police's belief that Norma had been murdered elsewhere.

So where had Norma's body been hidden? Suspicion still pointed firmly towards a local person. An outsider was hardly likely to return to the area. The old adage of 'a murderer returning to the scene of the crime'may have some truth, but returning with the body? And if the killer had taken Norma away, how had they done it? Cars were still a luxury and a rare sight on the Tang Hall Estate. If there had been a strange one driving around that afternoon, then it would not have gone unnoticed. Even to walk Norma out of the street would have been difficult. She was a well-known little girl, dressed in a bright white dress, surely someone would have taken notice and remembered - but no one had seen Norma that afternoon. At least, no one who was admitting to it. An appeal had gone out for anybody to come forward who had seen anyone acting suspiciously and where was the missing red shoe? A diligent search in the neighbourhood had failed to find it. Policemen had emptied dustbins and searched through fire ashes without success.

By Monday, the initial five and half hour postmortem examination by Doctor Sutherland at Wakefield showed the cause of death to be manual strangulation, an act requiring considerable pressure to be applied, even to a young child. There were no signs of sexual assault. A more detailed report was awaited in the hope that it would give an indication of the time of death.

On Tuesday, 24 September, Chief Constable Herman sped back from his holiday to join two Scotland Yard detectives, Chief Inspector Stevens and Detective Sergeant Kennedy.

The grass on the wasteland was scythed and sent for forensic examination, while hundreds of Tang Hall residents were interviewed. One tactic used was to ask each man and woman to illustrate how they would lift and carry a child. Still nobody admitted to having seen Norma on that Saturday afternoon.

Rumours were rife. Frightened mothers accompanied their children to school, although police discounted any connection to child murders in other parts of the country. The story of a local man being arrested proved to be false, but it persisted for many weeks and speculation that the body had been hidden in a manhole on the wasteland was quickly denied.

And then seven-year-old Peter Bellwood came forward saying that he had seen Norma on Saturday afternoon.

Sometime after 2.40 pm he had been throwing stones into the beck with a little girl he believed to have been Norma Dale. A man approached wearing a trilby hat and a dark, white-flecked overcoat, telling them to go away or they might be drowned. He then told the girl that he would buy her an apple and she took his hand and walked away. The boy assumed that he was her father. The police, however, were sceptical, as although Peter was certain that the girl was Norma, he said that she wore a brown coat and Norma did not own such a coat. The story obtained full publicity, but the man who Peter saw that afternoon never made himself known.

Norma's funeral took place on 26 September at St Hilda's Church with the investigation no closer to an arrest.

When the full pathological report was released it contained some startling evidence. As Norma left her home for the last time she was carrying a rice cake, given by her mother. The post mortem revealed that due to the rate of ingestion, it was apparent that she had been killed only a short time later, probably around 3 pm. When Frances Dale was walking Rawdon Avenue shouting for her daughter, she was already dead. Perhaps the killer could hear the mother's calls.

Other evidence was coming to light. Forensic tests had uncovered coal dust on the shoulder of Norma's dress. Frederick Glover's coal lorry had already been removed for closer inspection, but had the body been kept there overnight then a greater amount of dust would have marked the white dress. Coal dust might have been present in the grass so close to the lorry's regular parking position. The location of Norma's body during the nineteen hours that she was missing remains a mystery to this day. Newspapers at the time reported that the dress was wet when she was found and that it had rained during that Saturday night. Had she been outside all night? Indeed, had she lain in the grass through the night, and nobody, not even Fred Glover who had walked so close to her, had seen her. If not, then the killer had carried Norma's body in broad daylight and left her without being seen. Would anybody have taken that risk? If they had, then that person had a clear view of when the coast was clear. That person was a neighbour. Everyone was agreed that the ground was clear up until 8 pm on Saturday night when the search was in place; perhaps then, Norma had been taken there under cover of darkness.

This photograph of Norma was used extensively by the newspapers in their coverage of the case. Author's collection

At the inquest, the coroner, Colonel Innes Ware treated each witness as though they were suspects. He was firmly of the belief that the murderer was present in the courtroom and he made no secret of that belief. The police also held strong suspicions without the evidence to back them up. Colonel Ware summed up with these words:

> *A far as we have been able to carry out this matter, this enquiry has been exhaustive and we have done all we can, and there is no evidence on which the jury could make anyone party to the crime.*

So what motive could anyone have had for murdering such a young and innocent child? It had been suggested that this was simply a case of jealousy. That someone begrudged the Dales their bright, pretty daughter. Michael Duffy spoke out in 1986, believing that she had been killed because of something she had seen. During an interview with Frances Webb for the *Yorkshire Evening Post*, he said,

> *I was only young, but I can remember people saying that a lot of things were going on at the time. Men were going off with women that weren't their wives, and Norma possibly heard something.*

Could that have been the case? One other person certainly thought so. After seeing Duffy's interview, Norma's mother, Frances Dale, contacted the newspaper from her home in Leeds. She firmly believed that the police should have been looking for a woman. What's more, she knew the woman personally:

> *A married woman I knew told me she was having an affair with another man and Norma kept asking me about it. She had obviously overheard our conversation. She never missed a thing and I fear that she may have gone up to this woman, when her husband was there, and started asking her about it. I bet the woman grabbed her to stop her blabbing and may have accidentally killed her.*

Norma's tiny marker stone rests before that of her father's who died in 1974.
The Author

Had Norma Dale spoken to a woman in the street and could this woman have really grabbed her in broad daylight? Perhaps she was taken into a nearby house and there strangled until she died. Strangulation of a four-year-old child can be no accident. Murdered for asking questions about something she can have had no understanding.

The case remains open to this day. Somebody, somewhere, may know the truth.

Sources

Newspapers consulted at York Reference Library, The British Library and in private collections:

York Courant 1801
Yorkshire Gazette 1813-1920
Yorkshire Herald 1772-1908
(York) *Yorkshire Evening Press* 1905-1986
The Times 1829, 1908
The *Morning Herald* (London) 1829
Daily Mail 1908
Daily Telegraph 1908
York Herald 1800-56

Books and Resources

The Luddites, I Malcom (Archon: 1970)
Calendar of felons, March and July 1793, March 1801 + July and August 1800.
Burdekins Old Moore's Almanac 1898, (article on Jonathan Martin) by Mr W Cambridge FRHS
The life of Jonathan Martin, T Balston (Macmillan: 1945)
The Life of Jonathan Martin of Darlington, J Martin (Lincoln: 1828) 3rd edition.
All Year Round. Att. Charles Dickens (London: 1866)
Poverty, A study of Town Life, S Rowntree (London 1901).
Report on the prevalence of typhoid fever in York 1884, S W North (York: 1885)
The Retreat, Mary Glover (Sessions 1984.)
The Tukes of York, W & M Sessions (Sessions: 1971).
Yorkshire and the History of Medicine, Malcolm Parsons (Sessions 2002)
A History of the Police in England and Wales, T A Critchley (Constable: 1967)
'Police Reform in early Victorian York', R Swift (University of York: 1987) Borthwick Papers Vol 73.
The History of the NSPCC (NSPCC publication: 2000)
Baines's Directory (of Professions and Trades for York) 1823
White's Directory (of Professions and Trades for York) 1840
Kelly's Directory of York: 1901
Life in Regency York, Prudence Bebb (Sessions: 1992)
Vacation thoughts on Capital Punishment, Charles Phillips (Cash: 1856)
Crime and Punishment in England, Briggs, Harrison, Mc Innes, Vincent (UCL Press: 1996)
The Common Hangman, James Bland (London: 1984)
The Noble City of York, Ed: Alberic Stacpoole (Cerialis Press: 1972)
History of the Castle of York, T Cooper (London Elliot Stock: 1911)
'The Parish Register of St Mary Castlegate' (1705-1837) Ed: M Mulgrew (The *Yorkshire Archaeological Society*: 1971)
Poverty and Prejudice, Frances Finnegan (Cork University Press: 1982)
York: The Continuing City, Patrick Nutgens (Faber and Faber: 1976)
Report on the state of the City of York, T Laycock (Physician to the York Dispensary), (York: 1844)
York: a survey, Editors: Willmot, Biggins and Tillott. (The Herald Printing Works on behalf of the York Executive Committee: 1959)
A Tour through the Whole Islands of Britain, Daniel Defoe (London: 1724)
A History of Grays of York 1695-1988, WHC Cobb (York: 1989)

Acknowledgements

Many thanks to the staff of the York Reference Library, Doncaster Libraries, York City Archives, Borthwick Institute of Historical Research, Mr Tony Lawton of Grays Solicitors, York and to all those nameless people I have met on my travels and who helped me in countless ways.

Index

Acomb, 51, 55, 118
Allen, Dr Edward, 68, 70
Allen, Mary Elizabeth, 119
Allenby, Major, 145
Aram, Eugene, 9
Archbishop (of York), 42, 44
Arundel, William, 16
Askern, Thomas, 27, 28
Assembly Rooms, 21
Athelstan, King, 7
Atkinson, Mr, 43
Backhouse, James, 43
Banes, Mr (analyst), 118
Barclays Bank, 161, 162
Barker, Mrs, 133
Barker, William, 23
Barlby, 90
Barton, Elizabeth, 54
Beetham, Mr (of Leigh on Sea, 119
Bellwood, Peter, 171
Bennington, Helen, 144, 154
Bentley, Alderman (Sheriff), 108
Best, Dr, 41
Billington, Isabella, 14
Billington, John, 108
Bishopthorpe, 44, 45
Blain, Mrs, 67
Blake, Dr Baldwin, 42
Bordington, Elizabeth, 14
Boroughbridge, 56
Bower, Mr, 47
Bradley's Buildings, 137
Broadley, Mrs, 104
Brougham, Henry, 36
Brown, Thomas, 51
Brown, Wlliam, 27
Burlington, Lord, 21
Cade, John, 75
Calverley, Walter, 14
Campbell, Inspector James
    (NSPCC), 144
Campbell, Isabella, 59, 60, 61, 62
Carlton, Henry, 35
Carr, George
Carr, Mary, 130, 132121, 131, 132
Carr, John, 10, 39, 40
Castle Museum, 17
Chambre, Sir Alan (of Abbot
    Hall), 20-22
Charlton, Mr, 73, 74
Chatwin, Francis Plummer (and
    wife), 101, 102, 104
Children's Charter (1889), 135
Christie, Walter, 117
Churches, Chapels
    St Mary's (Bishophill junior), 50
    St Mary's Abbey, 7
    St Andrew's (Bishopthorpe), 45
    St Saviour's (Hungate), 89, 90
    Victoria Bar Chapel, 93, 95
    St Paul's (Heslington), 133, 134
    All Saints (Huntington), 159
    St Hilda's (Tang Hall), 171
Clark, Major, 34
Clarke, Reverend James, 133
Clayton, Mrs, 133
Clematis House, 158
Clifford's Tower, 12,18
Clitherow, Margaret, 12
Close, John (Lord Mayor), 86
Coates, James, 27
Cobb, Cecil, 114, 115, 119
Collingham, 119
Coilins, Daniel, 60
Connell, Edward, 128, 130-132
Connery, John, 96
Conolly, Wlliam, 15
Cook, Elizabeth, 14
County and Borough Act (1856), 78
Crees, Dora, 141,142, 145, 147, 148,
    150, 152, 154
Crombie, George, 145
Crombie, Norman, 137, 146

Crowther, Joseph, 25
Crummack, Mr, 62
Cubit, Sir William, 19
Curry, John (aka William
    Wilkinson), 19, 22-27, 37
Curry, Pat, 52
Dalby, John, 102, 104, 105, 106, 108
Dale, Cyril, 168, 169
Dale, Frances, 168, 171, 173
Dale, Norma, 167-173
Daniels, Herbert, 121, 124, 125, 126,
    131
Darling, Justice, 108
Davidson, James, 162
Davies, George, 117
Dawson, Joseph, 160-162, 166
Debtor's Gaol, 17
Defoe, Daniel, 17
Denham, Frank, 137-139
Denham, Mary, 137, 138
Deramore, Lord, 130, 132, 145
Dickens, Charles, 11, 37, 38
Dickson, (Alfred) Charles, 129,130
Dixon, Reverend, 44
Dodsworth, Benjamin, 166
Dodsworth Ralph Ernest, 161, 164, 165
Dove, William, 11
Draper, Dr, 147
Driscol, Daniel, 11
Duffy, Michael, 168, 169
Duke of York, Richard, 15
Eastwood, Mr P, 148
Ellis, Dr, 47
Ellis, Reverend Paul, 108
Evans, John, 165
Evelyn, Dr W A, 147, 148
Fern Cottage, 157, 159, 161, 164
Flood, Dr William, 106
Fowler, Jane, 63, 4, 65, 68, 70
Fowler, William (Old), 63, 64, 65, 66, 67
Fry, Elizabeth, 18
Fulford, 86
Gallagher, John, 95, 96, 97, 98
Gamble, Sarah, 88
Gascoigne, Sir Thomas (of Parlington)
Hall, 20
Glover, Fred, 170-172
Gowland (nee Norton), Jane (see also
    Norton, Hannah), 49, 51, 52, 54-56
Gowland Charles, 49-52, 54-56
Graham, Sir Robert, 20
Grinling, George, 165
Guildhall, 36, 62, 90
Gurney, Joseph, 18
Habit, Tom, 96
Hall, 20
Hall, Clarke, 145, 150-152
Hall, Edmund (aka Smith, James),
    101, 102, 104, 107, 108
Hall, Hannah, 101
Hall, John, 58, 60, 62
Hardcastle, Mrs, 67
Heslington, 121-123, 127, 133
Heslington Manor House, 128, 132
Hewitt, Harry, 111, 112, 114-120
Hewitt, Isabella, 110-112, 114, 116, 119
Hewitt, William, 110-112, 114, 116,
    117, 119
Higgins, Godfrey, 42, 43
Hildyard, Sir Robert D'Arcy (of
    Whinstead), 20
Hill, John, 25
Hobson, John, 117
Hodgson, Dr Brydges, 55
Holberry, Samuel, 19
Holmes (nee Liddle), Annie, 155, 157-160
Holmes, Francis, 155, 156, 158, 159,
    163, 164
Horsemonger Prison (London), 11
Howard, Nathaniel, 27
Hughes, Edward, 10
Hughes, Thomas, 85
Hunter, Dr, 39, 41
Huntington, 156
Hursley, Joseph, 47
Jackson, Hannah, 161

Jackson, Inspector (NSPCC), 138
Jackson, John, 51, 52
Jackson, William, 23
Jagger, John, 104, 105, 108
Jagger, Martha, 104
Johnson, Andrew, 72
Johnson, Elizabeth, 19, 22, 122
Kell, Edward, 35
Kemp, Mr, KC, 146, 148,
Kidd, Martha, 42
Kitchen, Mr, 127
Kivell (nee Conney), Mary, 93, 95, 96,
    97, 98
Kivell, James, 93, 96, 99
Kivell, Martin 93, 95, 96, 98, 99
Kivell, Mary Ann, 93, 98
Knowles, Job, 33
Knox, William, 163
Lámbert, Horatio, 87-90
Langan, Michael, 75, 76
Law, William, 30, 31, 35
Lawson, Francis, 118
Lawson, Richard, 145
Lawson, Sir John Grant, MP, 145
Leaf, John, 142, 144, 145, 148-150
Leetham's Flour Mill, 87, 88
Liddle, Gertrude, 104
Liddle, John,
Liddle, Thomas, 156-163, 165, 166
Linton Bridge, 117
London Society for the Prevention of
    Cruelty to Children, 135
Long, Arthur, 142, 143
Lowenthal, Mr (Solicitor), 161
Luddites, 23
Lund, Mrs, 161
Lyons, Mary, 77
Lyons, Thomas, 76,77
MacKay, Mr (JP), 139
March, Mr, 74
Margaret, Queen, 15
Marshall, Dr J, 88, 99
Martin, Fenwick and Isabella, 29
Martin, John, 29, 36, 38
Martin, Jonathan, 29-33, 35-38
Martin, Maria, 30-35
Martin, Richard, 38
Marwood, William, 12, 28
May, Olive Mabel (aka Smith, Nita),
    140-145, 147, 148, 150, 152, 154
Mayne, James, 15
McCarthy, Martin, 76
Metcalf, Thomas and Eliza, 55
Metcalf, William, 115, 116
Methley, Charles, 19
Mills, Hannah, 41, 42
Milner, Sir William (of Nun Appleton
    Hall), 20
Milvain and Gotrain (solicitors), 120
Moreland, Richard, 130
Municipal Boroughs Act (1835), 72
Municipal Corporations Act (1835), 72
National Society for the Prevention of
    Cruelty to Children (NSPCC), 137,
    142, 143-145, 148, 154
Nay, Mrs, 133
Nether, Poppleton, 139, 146
Nevison, John, 9
New Drop, the, 11, 23-25
New Earswick, 91
Newspapers: (mentioned/quoted in text)
    The Times, 11
    York Herald, 10,20, 85, 122
    Yorkshire Evening Press, 122,
        123, 125, 127, 130, 133
    Yorkshire Evening Post, 172
    Yorkshire Gazette, 12, 26, 27,
        28, 38, 74, 75, 78, 79, 82
    Yorkshire Herald, 148, 152, 154
Newton upon Derwent, 49
Nicholson, Caroline, 59, 60, 61, 62
North Eastern Railway Company
    (NER), 110, 117, 153
Norton, Colonel, 26
Norton, Hannah, 49, 51, 52, 55, 56

O'Greary, Father, 77
Oliver, Arthur, 158, 161, 166
Othick, Elizabeth, 64, 65, 66
Palmer, Elizabeth, 87, 88, 89, 90
Palmer, Mary Anne, 90
Panett, Bridgett, 97
Parker, Frank, 46-48
Parker, Frederick, 11
Parkin, Ernest, 163
Parkinson, Frederick, 102
Pearson, Matthew, 55
Percy, Sir Henry (Hotspur), 15
Percy, Sir Thomas, 15
Peter Prison, 33, 35, 36
Phillips, Charles, 11
Pierepoint, Henry, 108
Pinkney, Albert, 133
Pinkney, Arthur, 125, 126, 127, 134
Pinkney, Elsie, 126
Pinkney, Eva, 122, 134
Pinkney, George Richard, 128-130
Pinkney, John, 121, 124, 127, 129, 130, 132
Pinkney, John jr (Jack), 126
Pinkney, Madge, 125
Pinkney, Sarah, 121, 124
Poppleton House, 139, 140, 142-145
Policemen:
  Bain, Sergeant, 111
  Capstick, Inspector Thomas (CID), 169
  Carter, Chief Constable Cyril (previously Superintendent), 82, 169
  Carter, Constable, 72
  Catton, Police Constable William, 61
  Chalk, Chief Constable Robert, 73, 74, 77
  Cowton, Parish Constable Matthew, 75-77
  Denham, Detective Sergeant Frank, 89, 90, 100
  Duke, Constable Robert, 77
  Farmery, Constable, 124-127
  Haley, Chief Constable Stephen, 77, 78, 88
  Herman, Chief Constable Harry, 170
  Holmes, Constable William, 76, 77
  Kennedy, Detective Sergeant (Scotland Yard), 170
  Masterman, Inspector, 96, 97
  Morrell, Detective Inspector, 106
  Selby, Sergeant Charles, 105
  Smith, Captain, 72
  Southwood, Constable, 111
  Steel, Inspector, 98
  Stevens, Inspector (Scotland Yard), 170
  Thornton, Police Constable, 88
  Wand, Constable, 114
Prospect House, 129
Public Health Act (1872), 86
Public Houses/Inns:
  Barkers Hotel, 59
  Black Boy, 52
  Black Swan, 52, 54
  Bricklayers Arms, 64, 67, 68
  De Yarbrugh Arms (Heslington), 127
  Grey Marcia, now *The Poacher* (Acomb), 55, 56
  Hare and Hounds (Ricall), 90
  Lord Nelson (Nether Poppleton), 149
  McGregor's Dram Shop, 61
  Snainton New Inn, 58
  Sun Inn (Long Marston), 117, 118
  The Brown Cow, 94, 97
  The Jolly Sailor, 62
  The Spotted Dog, 96
  White Swan, 58
  Windmill Inn, 57
'Pudding Holes,' the, 62
Quinn, Alice, 64
Quinn, Thomas, 66
Redd, Mrs, 133
Reed, Robert, 59

Retreat, The, 40, 41 ·
Reynolds, Dr Harry William, 116, 138
Richardson, John, 52
Ridley, Mr Justice, 120
River Foss, 83, 85, 87
Roberts, Thomas, 23
Robinson, Charles, 54
Rowntree, Seebohm, 91
Rowntree's (factory), 84, 165
Rushworth, Cecil, 139, 141, 150
Rushworth, Charles George Golden, 139, 140, 144-146, 148, 150-152
Rushworth Sarah Catherine, 139-146, 148, 150, 152-154
Rust, William, 161, 164, 165
Rylett (nee Fowler), Jane, 63, 64, 65, 66, 67, 68, 70
Rylett, Thomas, 63, 66
Rymer, Mr (Under-Sheriff), 108
Sargent, John, 60, 61
Scott, Captain (of Filey), 139
Scott, Mr, 33
Severs, Thomas (of Heworth), 23
Shaftsbury, Lord, 135
Shakespeare, 15
Shaw, Michael, 26
Shearman, Mr Justice, 166
Shearsmith, George, 109
Shortt and Godley (solicitors), 120
Sullivan, Simeon, 75
Simpson, Charles, 87
Skelton, Hester, 53, 55
Smith, William, 23
Snell, Anne, 49, 51
St George's Field (Bedlam), 37, 38
St Peter's Vaults, 99
Stainthorpe, William, 35
Stamford Bridge, 49
Standish, Samuel1, 42
Station Hotel, 115
Stoddart, Dr, 127, 130
Stone, Fred, 109, 110
Stork, Matthew, 119
Streets and Districts:
  Alma Terrace, 102-104, 106
  Baille Hill, 26, 36, 37
  Baker Street, 121
  Bedern, 75-77
  Beedham's Court (Hagworms Nest), 85
  Bishophill, 49, 50, 144
  Bridge Street, 57
  Brunswick Terrace, Hungate, 92
  Burton Stone Lane, 7
  Castlegate, 59
  Castlegate Postern, 11
  Clarence Gardens, 7
  Clifford Street, 59, 108, 151
  Clifton, 86
  Dennis Street, 69
  Duncombe Place (Lop Lane), 36, 161
  East Mount Parade, 116
  Fishergate, 78, 127
  Foss Bridge, 7, 72
  Fossgate, 85
  Gale Lane, 118
  Garden Place, Hungate, 89
  Goodramgate, 76
  Heworth, 22, 86, 168
  Holgate Road, 167
  Hope Street, 93, 94, 97-99
  Hungate, 83, 85-87
  Jackson's Yard, 72, 73
  King Street, 60
  King's Staithe, 60
  Knavesmire, 7, 9, 10, 14
  Lord Mayor's Walk, 114, 115
  Lower Wesley Place (Hungate), 83
  Micklegate (Bar), 15, 16, 74, 109
  Nessgate, 60
  Newgate, 101
  Nunnery Lane, 93
  Oldsworth, 30, 31
  Ouse Bridge, 13

Pavement, 59, 88, 89
Paver Lane, 63, 64
Poppleton Road, 117
Queen's Street, 111
Rawdon Avenue, 167-169, 171
Shambles, the, 12, 85
Silver Street, 71
Skeldersgate, 85
St John's Terrace, 78
St Leonards, 14
St Saviourgate, 91, 99, 138
Stonegate, 145, 158, 163, 164
Swan Street, 85
Tang Hall, 91, 168, 170, 171
The Crescent, 109, 115, 116, 119
Thief Lane, 85
Tofts Green (House of Correction), 62
Tower Street, 12
Walmgate, 63, 68, 72, 91, 93
Water Lanes, 59, 60, 85
Wiggington Road, 39, 57
Sutherland, Dr, 170
Swinbank, Robert, 33
Taylor, Mr, 57
Taylor, Mr (coroner), 90
Terry, Alderman, 90
The Prevention of Cruelty to Children Act (1904), 137, 146
Thompson (nee Hardy), Annie, 158, 160, 161, 164
Thompson, John Raper, 161, 164
Thompson, Bielby, 34
Thompson, George, 140, 147
'Tin Pot Band' (rough music), 146
Topham, Major, 10
Trotter, William, 86
Tuke, Anne, 41
Tuke, Samuel, 41, 42
Tuke, William, 41
Turpin, Dick, 9
Tyburn, 7, 10, 14
Tyne, James, 76
Upper Poppleton, 49
Vickers, William, 42
Walker, Margaret, 163
Walker, Mary, 158, 161, 163
Walker, Robert, 158, 161, 163
Walker, Vincent, 28
Wanostrocht, Dr Vincent, 90
Ward, Mr, 127
Ward, Thomas, 46, 47
Ware, Colonel Innes (Coroner), 172
Waugh, Mr (Solicitor), 161, 163
Waugh, Reverend Benjamin, 135
Webb, Frances, 172
Wesley, John, 17
West, Elizabeth, 43
Westland, Mr, 76
Wheatfill, Edward, 12
Whitwell, Margaret, 61
Wilkinson and Lucas (solicitors), 114
Wilkinson, Colonel (JP), 145
Wilkinson, John, 47
Williams, Caleb and Isaac, 37
Wilson, Mrs (of Westow), 140
Women's Prison, 17
Wood, Mr JW (coroner)122, 131, 132
Wood, Mr JP (coroner), 62, 68
Wood, William, 52
Wragge, (Harry) Vernon, 145, 146
York
  Castle (Prison), 17, 22, 23, 48, 100, 112
  City Cemetery, 112, 113
  City Relay System, 168
  Civic Trust, 167
  Lunatic Asylum (Bootham Park Hospital), 39-44, 46-48, 95
  Minster, 31-34, 36, 38
  Railway Station, 107, 140, 141, 153, 155
  Rescue Home (The Shelter), 144, 154
Watchmen, 71